OPPORTUNITIES

in

Carpentry
Careers

OPPORTUNITIES

in

Carpentry Careers

REVISED EDITION

ROGER SHELDON

New York   Chicago   San Francisco   Lisbon   London   Madrid   Mexico City
Milan   New Delhi   San Juan   Seoul   Singapore   Sydney   Toronto

Library of Congress Cataloging-in-Publication Data

Sheldon, Roger.
    Opportunities in carpentry careers / Roger Sheldon. —Rev. ed.
        p.   cm.
    Includes bibliographical references.
    ISBN 0-07-147606-7 (alk. paper)
    1. Carpentry—Vocational guidance.   I. Title.

    TH5608.8.S54   2007
    694.023—dc22   2006028896

1 2 3 4 5 6 7 8 9 10 11 12 13 14 15 16 17 18 19   DOC/DOC   1 0 9 8 7

ISBN-13: 978-0-07-147606-5
ISBN-10:   0-07-147606-7

Interior design by Rattray Design

McGraw-Hill books are available at special quantity discounts to use as premiums and
sales promotions, or for use in corporate training programs. For more information, please
write to the Director of Special Sales, Professional Publishing, McGraw-Hill, Two Penn
Plaza, New York, NY 10121-2298. Or contact your local bookstore.

This book is printed on acid-free paper.

Contents

Preface

TODAY THE WORKING world is changing faster than ever. Technology and market forces continually trigger new business models and strategies as companies vie for competitive advantage. Increasingly in North America, we have information and service economies. We sell and promote things; we don't make them. Overseas trade deals by international conglomerates will undoubtedly shape a new world order over the next fifty years that few today would recognize.

Then we have the carpentry and building trades, which from the earliest times have been a cornerstone for human society. As carpentry advanced, so did the larger world. Of course, the trades are not immune to the winds of change, but it's clear that no matter what happens a generation or two from now, the world will need its builders. Foundations and frames still have to go up, and all of that takes planning, skill, know-how, and complex equipment. The United States alone now has more than three hundred million people, making it the world's third-largest country and mandating construction and maintenance of all the high-rises, office parks, retail establishments, neighborhoods, ships, bases, and parks that go along with a growing population.

Carpentry is not a static profession. Improvements in site development, building design, materials, and assembly continue to push the trade forward and call for dynamic, skilled workers. To stay on top, a carpenter must be committed to learning new skills and how new tools work. Training is crucial throughout the course of a worker's career, but you'll be able to adjust to most gradual advancements on the job. The steepest learning curve comes when you're entering the field, and that's where this book can help. You'll discover what you can expect on the job, how to lay the groundwork for a career in carpentry, how to approach training, and what resources to consult to take the next step.

With a few key aptitudes, some initiative, and the right training, you could continue the proud tradition of the skilled tradespeople who have always formed the backbone of our workforce.

1

An Ancient Craft

All across the United States and Canada today, skilled carpenters are measuring, sawing, leveling, and nailing wood in pursuit of their proud and ancient craft. They are installing tile and insulation board and placing composition shingles and aluminum siding. They are working with many new tools and materials to erect skyscrapers; build new homes; and construct bridges, boats, tunnels, and highways. Wherever people build, carpenters will be found.

A Noble History

It was the Romans who gave carpenters their name. In so-called "low" Latin, the word for wagon maker or chariot maker is *carpentarius*. The chariot makers who followed the Roman legions were skilled woodworkers. They were employed to build housing for the armies wherever they spent the winter or established a post.

When the Romans were among the Franks, these Germanic people watched the carpentarius framing bridges, repairing wagons, and building barracks. In ancient French, the Roman word was changed to *charpentier*, and when this word passed into the Anglo-Saxon tongue, it eventually became *carpenter*.

Carpenters make up the largest single group of skilled workers in the United States today. Today they hold more than 1.3 million jobs, according to the U.S. Bureau of Labor Statistics, and those numbers will steadily increase even as companies send other kinds of jobs overseas or eliminate them entirely through automation. Whether cities are expanding or revamping existing infrastructure, they need carpenters to do the work.

The carpenter has been a highly respected artisan since the dawn of civilization. With crude stone axes, early people built huts and enclosures to protect themselves from the weather and from enemies. Those individuals who excelled in the use of these ancient tools were highly respected members of society.

One of the earliest references to carpenters was in the story of Noah, who, according to Biblical legend, built an ark 300 cubits (about 450 feet) long to house two of each living thing.

Skilled carpenters sawed the cedars of Lebanon and erected Solomon's temple.

Skilled carpenters also helped build the classic temples of ancient Greece. These Greek builders used ingenious wood construction methods to create some of the many wonders of the ancient world. Carpenters also helped the Romans spread their civilization to the frontiers of Gaul and early Britain.

Carpentry for All Seasons

The first European colonists in America realized an immediate need for individuals skilled in the trades. Standing on the north shore of the James River, Captain John Smith of the Virginia Company looked about him and saw people from the English court with gilded lace on their clothing and fancy buckles on their shoes. Soldiers and adventurers abounded, but he found few men and women who were skilled with their hands and trained to fell trees, build stockades, whittle pegs, drive nails, mold candles, repair clothing, and perform the countless other tasks critical for survival in the wilderness.

He wrote to Sir Walter Raleigh in protest: "When you send again, I entreat you to rather send but thirty carpenters, husbandmen, gardeners, fishermen, masons, and diggers of trees' roots, well provided, than a thousand such as we have."

The Pilgrims who settled in New England also realized the value of carpentry skills. There were more carpenters on the Mayflower than persons skilled in any other craft.

As the young United States pushed westward, carpenters erected new towns, helped build railroads and bridges, and joined in building the ships that made the new nation the master of the seas.

Carpentry is truly a career that grows with America. As more and more Americans move from farms and small towns into big cities, the need for new housing, new industries, and new public facilities will require the skills of carpenters and other construction workers.

Carpenters create an amazing variety of things. A century ago, carpenters often spent their idle winter months building carousels and toys for youngsters. Almost two thousand of them worked on construction of Walt Disney World in Florida, and more than eight hundred help maintain the multifaceted park. Carpenters have helped build missile silos for our national defense, the Alaska Pipeline, major athletic facilities, and the spectator stands for presidential inaugurations. They have been part of the effort to rebuild Ground Zero in New York City and New Orleans in the wake of Hurricane Katrina, and they will stand at the ready to build, or rebuild, wherever need calls them. Carpentry has even figured in our relations with other countries. Developing nations seeking Peace Corps volunteers often ask for carpenters and others trained in construction work, as well as teachers and other specialists. One form of assistance these countries value highly is kits of carpentry tools that workers with basic skills can use.

Wood's Continued Importance

Wood has always been the primary material used in the majority of structures built in the United States. Few buildings of any kind are started without the use of wood. It is used in forms for pouring concrete, in staking out building sites, in scaffolding, in framing, and in finish work.

There are, in some cases, substitute materials, and carpenters work with these, also. But lumber and wood products still rank as the top choice for their structural performance and fine finish in housing and other light construction.

As a building material, wood has many advantages. It can be turned into many shapes without difficulty. It has great strength for its weight, and it has resilience, durability, and an attractive appearance.

Wood is one of the oldest building materials known to civilization, yet its versatility enables people to use it in a variety of new ways including as veneer, in laminations, and as free forms. It is even ground and mixed with other substances to be molded into tough new building materials.

Through glued lamination, lumber can be produced in many large sizes and shapes that cannot be cut freely at the lumber mill. Today, huge laminated wood arches add grace and beauty to churches, auditoriums, and bridges, where before only structural steel or reinforced concrete could be used.

Advanced fastenings and framing devices have increased wood's adaptability in construction and also increased the opportunities for employment in carpentry. Component building systems— building with preassembled parts instead of from rough materials— are increasing in use. In modular construction, whole sections of homes or other buildings are fabricated by machines and skilled workers before being assembled into master structures.

Through conservation practices, such as tree farms and new harvesting techniques, lumber producers ensure a constant supply of wood and wood products for the future. Research work done by the U.S. Forest Service and private industry has added considerably to the know-how of the construction industry and makes today's carpenter more versatile than ever before.

Today's Carpenter

The days when a carpenter needed only a hammer, a saw, and some nails are long past. Today's carpenters work with tiles, insulation boards, plastics, light metals, composition shingles, and acoustical materials. And these are only some of the building materials at their disposal.

The carpenter measures, saws, fits, and hammers. He or she uses levels, plumb bobs, planes, precision levels, chisels, and other hand or machine tools. The carpenter's tool chest will most likely contain hundreds of dollars worth of special-purpose tools and instruments. In addition, the carpenter's employer often supplies hundreds of dollars in power tools and equipment. Today's carpenter ranges from the "rough" carpenter, who erects basic frameworks, concrete forms, scaffolding, docks, and railroad trestles, to the "finish" carpenter, who must fit wood perfectly for hardwood floors, cabinets, and stairs and attach doorknobs and other hardware. Some carpenters do every type of carpentry work. Carpenters working in rural areas tend to be jacks-of-all-trades. They might prepare and pour concrete, paint, and even install plate glass. In cities, however, carpenters are more likely to be specialists—employed, for example, in the remodeling, repair, and maintenance of older buildings and industrial plants. Certain carpenters might install only acoustical panels. Others might focus exclusively on installing trim, fixtures, or doors.

One hot field for carpenters and the construction industry as a whole is remodeling, which was a $250 billion market in the United States in 2004. As home values increase over time, especially on the coasts where land is at a premium, many owners have chosen to remodel rather than move. Some of the biggest growth is in kitchen and bath remodels, which can mean brisk business for cabinet factories and small cabinetmakers but can also create work for carpenters on-site. Carpenters might prepare spaces for the hanging of new cabinets, move walls, build closets, or install partitions, doors, or windows.

Another growing field of activity is the installation of interior systems, including metal frame ceilings with various sizes of fiberboard and tile and elevated flooring that allows wiring, computer cables, and piping to run beneath.

In home building, carpenters begin at the foundation, helping to stake out the job; prepare the forms for concrete; and, when the foundation is set, build the structural framework—studs, joists, and rafters. They put in the subflooring and sheath the roof. If they are working on a frame house, they finish the outside walls with insulation, sheathing, and siding. They may even do the final roofing. Carpenters lay the floors, hang the doors and windows, cut and fit the baseboards and other trim, and build stairs and handrails. They set door locks and other hardware and build and install cabinets and other built-in features.

The *Dictionary of Occupational Titles*, compiled by the U.S. Department of Labor, lists more than three dozen different titles for the carpentry and joinery fields. A skilled journeyman carpenter can usually perform any of these varied jobs after a brief "postgraduate" indoctrination.

Outlook

Construction spending has grown at a record-setting clip in recent years, as the industry builds the roads, factories, office buildings, homes, and retail districts that people are demanding. U.S. construction spending for 2006 should top $1.2 trillion, or nearly 10 percent of the gross domestic product for the year. Canada's construction sector has shown similar gains, with spending estimated at C$164 billion for 2006. In the years to come, the sounds of hammers and power saws will continue to echo in new skyscrapers, churches, schools, and hospitals. The staccato of construction tools will be heard in new industrial plants and along thousands of miles of interstate highways. Large or small, each project will be put together by men and women trained in many craft skills.

The construction industry is one of the largest in the country by dollar volume, and it is growing. As our economy and population increase, the construction industry by necessity must expand, and carpenters are at the center of this movement. Construction requires a higher proportion of skilled workers—two out of every three—than almost any other industry. (Compare this ratio with manufacturing and transportation, where one in five workers is skilled.)

Carpentry is the leading skilled trade in the construction field, employing more than twice as many workers as the next ranking trade.

As a result, employment of carpenters is expected to increase as fast as the average of all occupations through 2014, according to the U.S. Department of Labor. Construction in particular will need many workers; contractors report having trouble filling all the openings they have for carpenters.

2

What It's Like on the Job

A CARPENTER'S WORKDAY does not consist merely of putting a hammer to a nail. As you'll see, the everyday work of a carpenter is as varied and complex as the tools in his or her toolbox.

The Workday

The traditional carpenter in the past dressed for the job in tough, durable overalls, usually of white duck or denim, with a detachable nail pouch at the waist. These were specially made overalls with straps and pockets to hold working paraphernalia—nails, hammer, pencils, measuring tape, screwdriver, and so on. The carpenter of days gone by wore a durable work shirt as well.

Today the wearing of sturdy clothes is still a common thread all carpenters share to some degree, but their tools, routines, and work environments vary widely depending on their tasks. Millwrights, for example, install and work on heavy industrial equipment using hydraulic lifts, precision measuring equipment, welding machines, and hydraulic torque wrenches. Pile drivers work on buildings, bridges, oil platforms, and other structures driving pilings, which might be metal, wood, or concrete. Cabinetmakers use tools the layperson might be more familiar with—table saws, jointers, and routers—but in large factories the tools can be computer-controlled and much larger than what we're used to seeing and using. Carpenters in these settings might specialize in one or two tasks, such as sanding or finishing.

Wherever they work, carpenters can expect a lot of noise, whether from heavy equipment, power tools, or other construction or factory work going on around them. Eye protection, hard hats, and safety shoes are necessary. The jobs generally require a fair amount of physical stamina (not necessarily strength), a working knowledge of structures and building principles, and, of course, good hand-eye coordination.

In the white-collar world, "tools" have become an abstract concept that translates roughly to job skills. For carpenters, however, tools are still very much indispensable physical essentials. Carpenters rely on them so heavily that many develop a special fondness for certain basic tools and can tell you when and how they were acquired. They will speak with pride of their tools' quality and usefulness. Recognizing this trait, building contractors encourage carpenters, millwrights, and other construction workers to use their own tools. However, contractors are still expected to supply the necessary power tools. All journeymen carpenters are skilled in the use of saber saws, radial saws, and other small power devices.

If it's the first day on a particular construction job, the carpenter usually brings tools along—clean, sharp, and orderly—in a toolbox. A carpenter takes great pride in his or her tools, protecting them from rust with frequent oiling and checking the handles to make sure they are securely fixed to their metal shafts. A mental inventory of the toolbox's contents is taken at the end of the day to make sure that all the tools are there. (See the glossary of tools, techniques, and concepts in carpentry at the back of the book.)

Most major contractors are also expected to provide facilities for locking up tools at the job site overnight. This way the carpenter simply goes directly to the toolshed when the workday begins. Vandalism is sometimes a problem in remote or poorly protected job sites, however, and the carpenter who has expensive tools usually takes special precautions. The contractor, nevertheless, is expected to provide a toolshed, and most carry insurance to cover losses of tools and equipment.

In some highway or bridge construction, however, the workers often have to take their tools home each night and return with them each morning. The trunks of cars or the backs of pickup trucks become their portable tool storage area.

On the job, carpenters work steadily to keep pace with their fellow workers but also get occasional work breaks. The breaks depend on the availability of building supplies, whether concrete is pouring, and other factors. Consequently, many carpenters bring their own beverages and snacks and take breaks when they can.

As you might have inferred from some of the above descriptions, carpenters are more and more becoming specialists. There are general carpenters still around, but they are less common than in years past as automation and preassembly have eliminated some tasks and as the labor market has evolved. Home construction, for example, used to be the domain of highly skilled craftspersons, including master carpenters. Now carpenters for new homes are much less experienced, nonunionized, and earn less than the average carpenter. These workers tend to be very young or are recent immigrants, which can occasionally lead to communication problems on the site and subsequent safety issues. While the housing market will ensure continued work in this area, carpenters who have completed an apprenticeship or other formal training will likely wish to set their sights on a more lucrative niche.

Supervisors

An important part of an apprentice carpenter's learning process is his or her on-the-job training. An apprentice is assigned to work under an experienced journeyman carpenter, so that he or she will pick up skills by watching and emulating. This journeyman is the apprentice's immediate boss.

The journeyman carpenter's immediate supervisor is the foreman—another experienced journeyman who directs the work crew of carpenters and indicates what is to be accomplished each day. Over the foreman is the superintendent, who supervises the work of all crafts and is answerable to the contractor.

Teamwork counts in building construction, where the job must be done on schedule. The carpenter works with engineers, architects, and subcontractors, as the job requires.

Time on the Job

Many members of the craft work in shops and mills where the workday is fixed (except for occasional overtime). Unless there are big orders to be completed on short notice, the cabinetmaker or millwright in such employment works a regular thirty-five- or forty-hour week. In building construction, however, the carpenter can often be expected to work hard for short periods when contractors are struggling to meet deadlines. Since contractors may have to pay penalties when they do not complete projects on time, they may sometimes require carpenters to work overtime.

Since some carpentry work is seasonal, and building supplies do not always arrive on schedule, there are days when there is no work. When carpenters, cabinetmakers, or millwrights are laid off or have finished work on a particular job, they may check in with their local union, if they are union members, to let the union business agent know they are available for other work. They then go on a waiting list, if there is one, or they can visit the union hall—usually early on a Monday morning—to pick up new jobs. Contractors learn to ask for specific journeymen with whom they have worked before. A good carpenter can nearly always find work.

If the carpenter is not a union member, he or she may scan the classified ads, call fellow construction workers for leads, or visit construction sites. The nonunion carpenter finds most of his or her work in residential construction, maintenance work, or small commercial construction, where union representation is usually weaker.

Some carpenters change employers each time they finish a construction job. Others alternate between working for a contractor and working as contractors themselves on small jobs. About 30 percent of carpenters are self-employed.

Special Circumstances

The working conditions of the construction carpenter have been described. Similar conditions exist for skilled workers under the broader definition of carpenter—pile drivers, dockworkers, shipyard carpenters, and so on.

There are situations, of course, where part of the workday involves getting to the job site, which might be by boat, by tramway to a mountaintop, or even by plane or helicopter to some remote spot.

Under any conditions, the carpenters, cabinetmakers, pile drivers, millwrights, and other allied workers perform gratifying, creative, and lasting work. For most of them, no two days are exactly alike. They can point with pride years later to a building, bridge, or highway they once helped to build.

There is a growing awareness among the general population of the important role played by carpenters and other building tradespeople in our society. In the days after September 11, 2001, when sympathy and respect for the manually skilled workers who keep our world moving were at an apex, New York mayor Rudolph Giuliani's office enlisted the help of volunteer carpenters and others to salvage a steel-beam cross from the wreckage and erect a memorial to all the 9/11 victims at Ground Zero. When a Franciscan priest blessed the new site in a ceremony shortly thereafter, a carpenter stood alongside a New York City firefighter, a police officer, an iron worker, and several others to pay tribute.

3

THE RIGHT STUFF: ATTITUDE, SKILLS, PAY

CARPENTERS, TO BE successful, must be able to work with their hands as well as their heads. They are creative persons who like to use specifications, drawings, and tools to create something new and useful. Carpenters find plenty of action and variety in their work. They take pride in their skills and in doing their jobs well.

The late novelist Edna Ferber had warm words for the carpenter in her book *A Kind of Magic*:

> There is a rare characteristic inherent in men whose guild or craft is that of carpenter. I have occasionally known and remonstrated with surly, unreliable, and careless workmen of just about all other crafts and trades. I never have known a genuine carpenter who was not prideful in his work; gentle, forthright, and humane in his nature. Carpenters are, mysteriously, likely to be men of intel-

ligence and integrity; they are at once visionary and realistic. Perhaps the working with wood has something to do with all this. Sawing, cutting, hammering, nailing, the scent of clean wood is always in his nostrils. Perhaps still lurking in the wood is something of the quiet fragrant forest whence it came. It just could be that the still-living tonic of the long-felled trees clears the workman's brain and steadies his nerves and makes his hand sure and deft. Carpenters talk little above the tap of the hammer, the buzz of the saw, but, when they do speak, they are likely to be unloquacious and dryly humorous. All this fancied explanation could be false—and probably is. Doubtless the fundamental explanation for the characteristics of the genuine carpenter is that he is descended from the carpenter who possessed all these qualities—the carpenter craftsman, Jesus Christ.

You don't need exceptional physical strength to be a carpenter, but you must be healthy enough to lift many types of building materials, agile enough to climb ladders and maintain a good balance on scaffolds, and tough enough to work under occasional adverse weather conditions. You should also have a high tolerance for noise; on a construction site, a carpenter hears the pounding of hammers and the buzz of power tools almost constantly.

Preparing for the Job

Although a high school diploma is not absolutely essential, it is highly desirable and still required for many apprenticeship training programs. Experienced apprenticeship instructors and vocational teachers find that aptitude, manual skills, and knowledge of basic mathematics can launch a young person into a carpentry-training program and on his or her way to success. In many areas, a high school diploma is not as important as a natural ability to work with tools and to understand and apply the rules of arithmetic.

However, in some areas where carpentry training is offered, the applicant for training must be a high school graduate or possess an education equivalency certificate. Transcripts of school records might be requested. Check with school officials for the requirements in your area.

Students entering the job market right out of high school without some plan for vocational or specialized training sometimes find the employment situation discouraging. Many of these graduates have serious skill deficiencies in three basic areas: communications, mathematics, and problem solving. An estimated half of seventeen-year-olds in high schools can't solve math problems that involve several steps to reach a solution. With math and problem solving of major importance in carpentry, it is vital that a person pursuing this vocation give special attention to learning basic math while in school.

The young person with a serious interest in carpentry must focus on long-range goals and not be tempted to forego training for quick money in some other job that can be more easily learned. A philosopher once said, "The man who has a trade has an estate." He was not speaking of real estate, but rather underscoring the fact that people who have specialized knowledge, skills, and experience have more than money. They have a guarantee of future income. Their vocation becomes a valuable asset.

Moving Up in the World

Future carpenters can generally undertake an apprenticeship at age seventeen in the United States or age sixteen (or upon completion of the tenth grade) in Canada. Some states and regions require that a worker be eighteen before starting as an apprentice. There is no upper age limit, so people can apply in their twenties, thirties, and so on.

Once you become a journeyman—a full-fledged carpenter—you may work as a journeyman all your life and be assured of a vocation that is always in demand. There is no official retirement age. The age of retirement depends upon the individual, the employer, and the individual's ability to do the work well.

The journeyman carpenter also may elect to move to other jobs, such as estimator, inspector, foreman, or superintendent—or even to the ownership of a contracting business of his or her own.

White-collar workers in the United States now outnumber blue-collar workers. Automation and increased technology have reduced the number of unskilled workers needed in many plants and industries. The most experienced and skilled industrial workers are kept on until last, but even they sometimes are laid off, as machines perform more complex tasks. Carpenters and their fellow construction workers, however, will continue to be essential because of the on-site nature of much of their work. Society will always need builders.

Along with this continued need for skilled craftspeople has come a rise in the social status of the carpenter. In studies made by a group of sociologists over a forty-year period, carpenters rose from sixteenth place to eleventh place in preferred occupations.

Pay Scale

One big advantage in learning to be a carpenter is that you draw pay from the first day you begin training as an apprentice. Once you are accepted in an apprenticeship or preapprenticeship training program, you are both a student and an employed worker.

In most areas, the apprentice's starting wage is approximately 50 percent of the journeyman wage scale, and the wage is increased periodically, usually every six months, until the apprentice is earning 90 to 95 percent in the fourth and final year of apprenticeship training.

To find out what the pay is in your particular area, you need to know the current wage scale of journeymen carpenters, at what percentage of the scale apprentices are started and advanced, and how many months are required for each period of advancement. Depending on the region and the type of carpentry being done— pay for residential work is lower, while millwrights get paid very well—the union wage for a journeyman could be anywhere from $15 an hour to $30 an hour. Your local carpenters' union office, which you can locate through the United Brotherhood of Carpenters and Joiners of America's website at www.carpenters.org, can give you this information. From the home page, click on "Local Contacts."

Carpenters, whether union and nonunion, earn a median hourly salary of $16.78, or about $670 for a forty-hour workweek. But the figure rises for certain sectors, such as nonresidential construction ($18.70) and is significantly higher when one considers only the median salary for union carpenters. The top 10 percent of all carpenters earn more than $28 an hour. In 2004 the U.S. Department of Labor calculated carpenters' median annual salary at $38,250. Fringe benefits paid by an employer (hospitalization, retirement, and so on) sometimes add to the take-home pay of union carpenters.

Most carpenters can expect to average forty hours of work a week, though these hours do vary somewhat according to season and weather. In the summer a busy workweek might stretch to fifty hours, while winter schedules often entail considerably fewer hours. (Under most union contracts, carpenters receive overtime pay for all work over either thirty-five or forty hours, depending upon what has been negotiated.) In addition, the carpenter receives overtime premium pay for all work outside of normal working hours and premium pay if he or she does hazardous work. Often, particularly when working under a contract or for an employer year-round, carpenters also receive health and welfare benefits, pension benefits, and paid holidays. Under some union contracts, carpenters can acquire credits toward vacation pay from contractor associations. Maintenance carpenters employed on a year-round basis can expect vacations and holidays with pay.

Union workers in skilled trades sometimes draw criticism for the high wages they command. On an hourly basis, construction workers, including carpenters, are indeed well paid. Yet the rate looks less sensational when broken down into its parts. In the spring of 2007, a journeyman highway carpenter in Denver, Colorado's Carpenters Local 55 received $29.73 in total compensation. Yet that rate includes:

Health insurance	$4.80/hour
Pension	$1.50/hour
Training incentive	$1.00/hour
Vacation pay	$.85/hour
Annuity	$.85/hour
Apprenticeship	$.40/hour
International training	$.04/hour
Labor management cooperation committee	$.02/hour
Total	$9.46/hour

When these benefits and obligations aren't rolled in, as most are not when quoting a salaried worker's annual income, the carpenter making $30 an hour receives a base pay of just $20.27; that's about two-thirds of the initial figure. In addition, the labor can be extremely challenging and physically demanding, and workers get paid only for the hours they actually work. In other words, the carpenter's annual income is not what it would be if steady work were available throughout the year. But that cannot be relied upon. When the weather turns nasty or cold and job sites shut down, the carpenter's earnings stagnate unless he or she can find alternate work, which can often be out of town. April through November are the busiest months for carpenters.

Fortunately, the number of carpenters who are able to work year-round has increased in the past five years. Preassembly of some materials in shops has diminished weather vulnerabilities. And when carpenters are able to work year-round, it's possible for them to earn $50,000 or more. Carpenters expect some loss in pay while changing from one building project to another or during layoffs because of seasonality. However, steady work is usually guaranteed for the most competent workers because they are so valued by employers.

Labor Supply

Unions and contractors have had to scramble to find new ways to attract qualified workers to enter the carpentry field. The chairman of a Louisville, Kentucky, construction company summarized the problem in a 2006 article in the journal *Business First of Louisville*: "Mom and Dad Want Kids to Work on Computers, Not with Their Hands." A business development director working for a general contractor in the same area expressed similar sentiments in that same story: "The construction industry has really taken a black eye over the past five or ten years, and it's only getting worse. More and more young people are pushed to get a college education, and, as a result, construction is a tough sell." Companies relying on carpenters have coped with the problem in a couple of different ways. Some companies are partnering with high schools to introduce students at an earlier age to the trades and the workers who proudly practice them through internships and preapprenticeships. Some unions are playing up the good pay and lifelong satisfaction and skills a career in carpentry provide. And both sides are looking to unskilled workers interested in advancement to train and place in skilled positions.

Such changes mean a golden opportunity for anyone who likes to see physical results from thoughtful, diligent effort. (See Appendix A for books, magazines, and websites for more resources, advice, and information on carpentry.) Once seen as lesser work, skilled labor has taken on a new respectability as college educated white-collar workers have discovered their jobs are as easily outsourced and downsized as those of blue-collar workers a generation ago, and that the buzz of saws and feel of wood offer a sense of purpose and authenticity lacking in the static, artificially lit cubicle cities that office employees know too well. Carpenters know that their jobs are more secure than those of a good number of white-collar workers. And carpenters have an advantage in that their rank-and-file members are already well organized and prepared to defend their jobs in a way unfamiliar to most office workers.

As competition in construction has become more cutthroat in nature and companies either can't or won't spend money on training their workers, the United Brotherhood of Carpenters and Joiners has stepped in with enhanced training programs that will keep its membership on the forefront of carpentry work for at least the next generation. In fact, its $22 million "train-the-trainer" facility is educating new instructors to run 250 programs throughout North America.

4

GETTING STARTED

IF YOU HAVE ambition and an aptitude for carpentry, a high school education is desirable but not absolutely essential. In nearly all carpentry training programs, however, you must have successfully completed at least two years of high school.

Today, there are so-called preapprenticeship programs sponsored by both public and private agencies that help a person brush up on language and math basics. Such programs can be especially valuable for those who left school before graduating. In recent years, employer organizations and unions have relaxed the educational requirements somewhat so that more young people, particularly applicants without high school diplomas, will have a chance to acquire a vocation.

Nevertheless, a high school diploma or GED would be an asset in achieving advancement in the industry, and high school mathematics is essential. Mechanical drawing and shop courses also offer long-range advantages.

In any case, it will be difficult to obtain sufficient training and experience in carpentry outside an apprenticeship training program. These programs are usually cosponsored by labor and management groups under joint apprenticeship training committees.

The National Joint Carpentry Apprenticeship and Training Committee, a labor and management group that works with the U.S. Department of Labor, prepares and approves apprenticeship standards for carpenters as well as all the other various specialties included in the carpentry trade. The purpose of these standards is "the establishment and maintenance of high standards of the trade and the development of skill and knowledge of the apprentice." They are also designed "to ensure the continuance of the development techniques, standards of practice, and workmanship, to give vitality to them, to promote uniformity of practice . . ." These standards are considered as basic requirements for journeymanship, regardless of local requirements or conditions.

One section of the standards stipulates that an applicant must:

- Be a minimum of seventeen years of age
- Complete an application form
- Provide reliable documentation to substantiate skill, knowledge, and experience

That is all. So a high school diploma is not required, but certainly it would be an excellent way of satisfying a local labor-management training committee.

In Canada the standards are much the same but are set by the Canadian Council of Directors of Apprenticeship for all trades to ensure consistent capabilities among workers between provinces.

High School

The traditional courses that prepare a young person for a career in carpentry are:

• **Mathematics.** A good comprehension of basic mathematics is essential. Knowledge of how to reduce fractions to their lowest terms and how to multiply and divide numbers with decimal points is required for most apprenticeship qualifying tests in this vocation. You may be able to forget some of the so-called "new" and theoretical math, but you must be prepared to figure the amount of building materials needed for a construction job. You must learn something of simple geometry, so you can determine the pitch of rafters, for example, or work with data obtained by a transit survey.

• **Mechanical drawing and industrial arts.** Many high schools are making changes in their vocational training curricula, placing less emphasis on what might be considered do-it-yourself projects, such as creating broom holders and bookshelves, and putting more emphasis on an overall understanding of the construction industry. Mechanical drawing and drafting are becoming part of this overall training course.

A carpenter is expected to be able to read blueprints. He or she gets such training during the apprenticeship, but the better prepared a young person is to start carpentry apprenticeship training, the more time he or she will have to absorb the more difficult elements of carpentry.

Generally speaking, high school industrial arts courses will help young people discover whether they want to be carpenters by exposing them to some of the basics of working with tools. However, this exposure cannot be considered training in the craft itself.

• **Other high school courses.** Although no high school courses except mathematics, mechanical drawing, and industrial arts are directly related to carpentry, it is important to realize that employers and labor-management training groups look favorably upon the young person whose overall high school record reflects a variety of interests and talents.

Trade School

There are a good many vocational training schools spread all across the country that offer courses in carpentry. There are also correspondence courses in the trade. And many mail-order publishers offer sets of books that contain the basic instruction for carpentry. Some of these courses and books can be used to supplement instruction in preparing for the carpentry trade, but you must remember that there is no substitute for experience—using tools of the trade—in learning a skilled craft.

The best training in carpentry, therefore, comes from working alongside skilled journeymen and supervisors on the job, which is what an apprenticeship training program offers.

While it is possible to go to a trade school that teaches carpentry and get a certificate that makes you eligible for some jobs in the field, such jobs are limited. When skilled carpenters are needed, most major contractors will hire graduates of apprenticeship training programs. Some private career schools or trade schools take pride in the fact that they graduate students in fewer than two years. Many technical schools have courses that last 102 weeks. Union-oriented schools, however, contend that the higher-paid union apprentice is much better served with the four-year apprenticeship program.

What to Do Without an Apprenticeship

During the 1970s, in order to offer a helping hand to those young people who could not otherwise bridge the gap between limited education and craft jobs such as carpentry, the federal government launched the first of its manpower training programs. Under these programs, funds are made available to sponsoring organizations to operate preapprenticeship training programs. Young people with insufficient education in reading and arithmetic are enrolled in classroom courses in more than a dozen training centers and are paid small amounts while they study. The goal is that when they finish preapprenticeship training, they will be sufficiently prepared to begin apprenticeship training.

The preapprenticeship programs to date have experienced many dropouts. Young people who are not otherwise prepared for apprenticeship, but who stick to their studies while classmates drop by the wayside, will undoubtedly find opportunities in apprenticeship training waiting for them later on.

Preapprentices are paid while they are undergoing their training. Sometimes it is the minimum wage, while in some areas it is a percentage of a journeyman's pay, usually slightly above the minimum wage. Under some preapprenticeship programs, enrollees undergo a test period or probationary period of two weeks. This helps the trainer determine how sincere the apprentice is in wanting to get into apprenticeship.

In a few instances, preapprentices are paid only a flat salary, and in some cases they are provided health and welfare benefits under a union contract just like their journeyman teachers.

Assisting Journeyman Carpenters

The ratio of apprentices to journeyman carpenters is controlled in some areas by a joint commission of representatives of the local unions and state apprenticeship board, and by labor-management agreements. A ratio of one to three is common in some areas and one to five in others. According to the *National Standards Manual*, these ratios should be determined by the local needs.

In some areas there is strong competition for the available apprenticeships. The young person who wants to enter carpentry apprenticeship should find out whether there is a waiting list and, if so, how long it is. Sometimes a young person who aspires to be a carpenter can take a nonunion job as a carpenter's helper—which is classified as unskilled labor—until an opportunity to enter apprenticeship opens up. However, the union does not recognize the job classification of "carpenter's helper," and such work does not replace formal apprenticeship training.

Why Apprenticeship?

Apprenticeship training is like playing on the scrub team before you're ready for the varsity, like pitching in the bush leagues before you make the majors, like serving an internship before you become a doctor. You would not want your home or your school built by amateurs. You want experts who know how much stress a ceiling beam will take or who can adequately weatherproof a structure against winter winds and summer rains.

Apprenticeship training as a means of passing on craft skills goes back centuries to early recorded history. It is still practiced to some extent in many trades—for example, in the so-called "needle trades" of the garment industry. Although it is not as formalized as it is in the crafts, such training also exists for copilots to become senior pilots of airlines, among instructors hoping to become professors, and among countless other professional groups. It has, through centuries of experience, proven to be the surest way to prepare a young person for the building and construction trades. See Appendix B for the contact information of government apprenticeship offices in the United States and Canada.

5

CAREER OPTIONS

THE MOST FAMILIAR work classifications in carpentry are carpenter, cabinetmaker or mill man, and millwright. There are others, including resilient-floor layers, interior systems installers, lathers, bridge and dock carpenters, pile drivers, wood turners, and boatbuilders.

Under the jurisdiction of the United Brotherhood of Carpenters and Joiners of America, there are more than three dozen classifications in North America. Some are industrial jobs, some are considered unskilled, and some are semiskilled. There are, for example, thousands of lumber and sawmill workers who are members of the Carpenters Union, and many of their jobs require little or no advance preparation or training before going to work as full-fledged employees.

We are concerned here only with those jobs that require apprenticeship training to either a full or limited extent and that offer good pay as a journeyman. Let us examine them.

General Carpenter

The largest number of carpenters is in construction work (compared with maintenance, remodeling, and other related occupations). These are the do-all craftspeople who are skilled in "rough" work, such as concrete-form building, and in "finish" work, such as installing cabinets and hanging doors.

As circumstances and ambitions permit, carpenters can devote their careers to a specialty or to general work. It depends upon their personal preferences and abilities whether they work at rough framing or forming; decking or roofing; precision layout with blueprints and instruments; or finishing, such as installing partitions, wallboard, stairways, windows, and doors. There are also many types of construction to choose from—houses, office buildings, factories, warehouses, theaters, shopping centers, and others.

The largest number of construction carpenters—an estimated 60 percent—go into housing construction. As more and more people have moved to suburban areas over the past fifty years, the nation's demand for new housing has surged. The beginning carpenter should be warned, however, that there is a tendency in this critical area for contractors to hire many so-called "jackleg" carpenters for the semiskilled rough work. Home construction sites are so varied in size and geographic distribution that they often present problems for union organizers seeking to enlist members. In areas where union membership is not strong, wages tend to be lower than in well-organized areas.

Generally, construction carpenters share hard but satisfying work. It is physical work, often out-of-doors. For those who like to travel, carpentry skills offer an opportunity to go to the many different areas of the nation and world where such skills are needed.

The carpenters, in such cases, obtain clearance to transfer from their local union to the local union in the area to which they move.

Although the age of wooden ships is long past, general carpenters *are* employed in today's shipyards—building support structures, making repairs, doing trim work, and performing many other tasks. They are also employed in highway construction and bridge building.

Many carpenters find work in remodeling, a growing niche that accounts for about 10 percent of overall construction spending today. Carpenters can expect the amount of remodeling work to increase as baby boomers retire in greater numbers and choose to pay for improvements rather than do them themselves. The market is big enough that many carpenters specialize in remodels and sometimes in specific rooms. High-end remodels are driving the market, and carpenters need to be skilled in finish work and able to complete jobs quickly, especially in essential rooms such as kitchens and bathrooms.

Maintenance offers another opportunity. Most large industrial plants have either full-time construction craftspeople to perform repair and maintenance tasks or contractual arrangements with outside firms to perform such work. However, construction is still the major pursuit of the general carpenter.

Now that we've covered some of the many options available to a general carpenter, let's examine the jobs of some specialists.

Cabinetmaker

Mill-cabinet work is a highly skilled occupation that requires both patience and precision. Once a craft of small shops and independent tradespeople, today it is also an assemblage of craftspeople employed by outside work crews, mills, and factories. In these factories, modern tools and jigs and assembly-line methods allow for the continuous production of high-quality residential, office, and commercial fixtures.

A career in cabinetry requires patience and exacting skill. It requires much indoor work and offers a variety of specializations. Because the work is indoors, it offers a greater opportunity for steady work than do many general carpentry tasks.

Today, skilled cabinetmakers and millworkers are employed in prefabricating cabinet units and fixtures in plants that are often far away from the site of the cabinets' or fixtures' final installations.

Millwright

Another craftsperson of precision is the millwright, who is concerned with the precision fitting of machinery to specifications within thousandths of an inch. It is the millwright who installs and aligns heavy industrial machines so that they operate efficiently. He or she uses micrometers (a precision measuring device) and electronic sensors to install machinery and to connect power-unit shafts to operating equipment.

The millwright installs conveyor systems, escalators, electric generators, and even the big cyclotrons of nuclear physics. A nuclear power plant is huge, but millwrights align its working units to specifications similar to those in fine watchmaking.

Though millwrights constitute only a small part of the membership of the United Brotherhood of Carpenters and Joiners of

America (the union covering their jurisdiction), they are an elite and skilled group of workers.

Apprentice millwrights spend 144 hours in classes per year, studying the use, maintenance, and calibration of delicate instruments. Their on-the-job training exposes them to the installation of all types of light and heavy metal equipment and machinery. Although much of their work is done indoors, millwrights often work outdoors to install conveyors and power-plant equipment.

Resilient-Floor Layer

The installation of fine carpeting, composition materials, and polymer or plastic materials is the work of the resilient-floor layer. There is apprenticeship training in this particular skilled trade in a growing number of cities.

In Chicago, for example, apprentices in the resilient-floor program spend forty-five days in the classroom studying the properties and characteristics of each of the many types of available flooring materials.

These apprentices learn to scribe, cut, fit, lay out, and seam tile and sheet stock in a variety of patterns under many different conditions. They learn the skill of binding, cutting, sewing, taping, cementing, and laying carpet as well as how to read blueprints and draw plans. Resilient-floor-layer apprentices also learn how to estimate the square yardage required for a flooring job. Almost all of their work is indoors, with perhaps the exception of the installation of so-called indoor-outdoor carpets, which may require outdoor work on commercial, institutional, or residential properties.

Pile Driver

The person who operates the big puffing and pounding machine in the foundation work for a new high-rise building is the pile driver. Pile drivers sometimes work almost entirely alone, once the piles (long shafts made of wood, steel, or concrete used to support great weights) are placed in position for driving into the ground.

The work is outdoors, and it requires steady concentration when the pile driving is under way. Opportunity for work in this specialty is somewhat limited because only a small number of pile drivers can be employed at one time at a job site. The pile driver must work closely with surveyors and engineers, driving their piles to particular depths. At times, rock formations and substrata complications test the knowledge and skill of the pile driver. Pile drivers must learn, by experience and training, the stress and tolerance of the materials with which they work.

Shipwright

According to the dictionary, a shipwright is "one whose work is the construction and repair of ships," but that definition is really an oversimplification.

Years ago, when all ships were built of wood and were much smaller than today's vessels, the story was simpler than it is today, though the principles and many of the skills remain the same. Shipwrights now share their work with metalworkers, but they have retained their responsibility for "shaping the ship," and they still use many of the traditional craft skills of shipbuilding.

Shipwrights follow blueprints and ships' plans, and they sight, plot, and mark reference points and lines on docks and ways (the inclined structures upon which ships are built or launched) to maintain proper alignment of vessels during construction or repair. For this work, they use transits, plumb bobs, tapes, and levels. They build keels and bilge blocks, cradles, and shoring for supporting ships in dry dock or on ways.

Shipwrights also position and secure blocking and other structures on dock platforms, according to ship's blueprints, and align vessels over blocks. They establish reference points and lines on a ship's hull for locating machinery and other equipment in accordance with a ship's alignment and shape.

If it is required, shipwrights shape, finish, and install wooden spars, masts, cargo booms, and boat booms. They may also fabricate and install furring pieces, aprons, uprights, and other wood framing in a ship, and trim wooden frames and other timbers. They spike or bolt metal fittings, plates, and bulkheads to the wooden parts of a ship and are responsible for building the staging and scaffolding needed for work on ships.

In most shipyards, shipwrights have a four-year apprenticeship. Their training includes all the areas covered by carpentry apprentices, but they must also learn to work with curved and shaped surfaces in addition to the usual straight and square shapes.

Work in a shipyard appeals to certain types of carpenters. Those who would be happy doing nothing but shop work would probably not find shipbuilding to their liking. Here, workers perform their tasks in the shop and also out on the ways, under ships, and high in the air above the ways.

Besides the standard modern power tools, shipwrights' tools include the traditional broad axe, adz (a cutting tool used to shape wood), and caulking equipment. Their tool kits are a mixture of ancient and modern implements.

Other Occupations

In addition to those occupations already listed, a carpenter-trainee can become an acoustical tile installer, a carpenter-welder, or a dock worker. He or she may even become a deep-sea diver; such individuals are employed in the installation of boat docks and other waterfront facilities and in the erection and operation of offshore oil-drilling rigs.

Some persons in the trade even find employment as woodcarvers and as wood-inlay specialists. Such occupations, in most cases, are outgrowths of the basic skills acquired in a general apprenticeship training program.

6

CARPENTRY PROS AND CONS

I HAVE TOUCHED upon some of the disadvantages of carpentry—the seasonal layoffs, the occasional work hazards, and, in some instances, the lack of long-range financial security. I have also indicated that much has been done to overcome these disadvantages. Before another decade has passed, it may be that only a small minority of craftspeople will endure some of these disadvantages. By way of review, let's take a look at the "cons" of carpentry, then sce how the "pros" of the profession weigh against the disadvantages.

Cons

Carpenters need to be aware of the downsides of their work as well as what is being done to remedy them.

Work Cycles

In 1968, a Presidential Commission on Seasonality in Construction was established. The panel—which included government, industry, and labor representatives—studied the methods used by other nations, especially Canada, to overcome seasonal work stoppages. They also investigated ways in which materials and supplies could be programmed to arrive at construction sites on time. They were also concerned with methods of overcoming traditional policies of construction financing, whereby funds are often made available in the spring or fall, when they might just as easily have been made available at another time of the year.

Technological advances of recent years have produced building materials that can be used at higher and lower temperatures than before; prefabrications that can be made indoors and moved to all-weather erection sites; and items such as space heaters and plastic canopies that protect workers from the elements.

Because of these studies and advances, seasonality should be a less costly problem in the future. Nevertheless, at present the loss of work time due to bad weather remains an important consideration in the building trades, as well as the fact that every construction job spans two to three years at most. About 40 percent of construction workers have work fewer than fifty weeks a year.

Risky Business

Statistics show a marked decrease in on-the-job accidents in the building and construction trades in recent years. In 1997 construction workers suffered 9.5 injuries per 100 employees. In 2003 cases of work-related injury and illness had dropped to 6.8 per 100 full-time construction workers, a welcome change and a major improvement over 1990 data, when injury rates had spiked to 14.1 per 100 workers. Hazards certainly do exist, though, and apprentices in the industry are warned to wear safety equipment and to practice safe working habits at all times on the job. The 6.8 figure for 2003, however, is still significantly higher than the 5.0 rate for the entire private sector. Workers who are employed by foundation, structure, and building exterior contractors experienced the highest injury rates.

The drop in injury rates is attributed to an ongoing emphasis on worker safety, as mandated by the Federal Occupation and Safety Act of 1970, which focuses on injuries that result in "lost time, restriction of worker motion, loss of consciousness, or medical treatment beyond first aid." In addition, the Construction Safety Act of 1969 and the Federal Occupational Safety and Health Act were designed to increase federal safety inspections on major construction projects and to establish safety standards at the state and local levels.

Fortunately, throughout the United States, there are laws providing unemployment compensation benefits for persons disabled by work injuries of long duration. Unfortunately, these jobless benefits vary all over the nation—from a high percentage of normal income in states like Hawaii and Washington to a figure below the poverty level in Alabama and Mississippi. Legislation has been proposed in the past to standardize unemployment compensation throughout the United States, and labor unions and other groups have supported it.

In any case, a carpenter who is laid off by work injury, work stoppage, or some other cause may apply for either unemployment compensation or disability benefits through state and local employment agencies.

Canadian citizens can apply for employment insurance benefits through the national government. The standard rate covers 55 percent of average earnings capped at $413 per week. Applicants can get more if they are in a lower income bracket and have children.

Pros

Some of the advantages of being a carpenter include health and welfare benefits as well as the ability to pick up extra work during slow seasons.

Health and Welfare Benefits

Today, most carpenters and other workers in the building and construction trades are covered by Social Security. Most full- and part-time workers in the industry are on payrolls that deduct Social Security taxes from their wages.

This is a great improvement over the situation in the late 1930s, soon after the Social Security Act was passed. It took many years of work on the part of the Social Security Administration, labor unions, and other groups to achieve this form of security for workers in the building and construction trades.

Because of such protection, today's carpenter can look forward to retirement at an earlier age than before. Social Security benefits are usually not enough, but they do offer a steady retirement income that was absent a few decades ago. In 1971, to supplement such income, the United Brotherhood of Carpenters and Joiners of America established the Carpenters Labor-Management Pension Fund, which is designed to offer its members continuous pension coverage, wherever they work, be it in the United States or Canada.

Many local unions and district councils of this organization have negotiated pension programs with local management.

*One of the long-sought goals of the construction industry has been portable pension protection. As things once stood, construction workers, who were employed by a firm or contractor that covered them with a pension plan, could not take this pension protection with them when they moved to another employer. The plan was not transferable. However, under pro-rate agreements that the carpenters' unions are currently signing with various pension participants, many carpenters are now able to change employers without losing pension protection.

Side Jobs

Carpenters can pick up occasional odd jobs and supplement their incomes. During seasonal layoffs, some carpenters take on remodeling jobs or home repairs. Others turn their skills to financial advantage by creating furniture, cabinets, and other household items.

Unions

Essentially, a labor union is formed by workers to improve their wages and working conditions and to establish job security. Unions seek to achieve such advantages by negotiating contracts with the members' employers.

The expense of having full-time union representatives, attorneys, and research workers is covered by dues paid by union members. The union members can judge for themselves what job advantages they get in relation to the amount of dues they pay. Since the union worker puts in fewer hours on the job because of longer vacations and added holidays, the compensation difference is usually greater when measured in terms of total compensation-per-hour actually worked.

As previously mentioned, there are areas where carpenters are not sufficiently organized to negotiate working arrangements with management. In such situations, carpenters working in these areas must judge for themselves the present and long-range advantages of union membership.

7

THE PATH TO JOURNEYMAN

AN APPLICANT FOR apprenticeship training must normally be at least seventeen years old. Some states will not permit anyone below the age of eighteen to work in construction because of hazardous-work laws. In these states, on-the-job training cannot begin until age eighteen. There is no upper age limit. An applicant must convince the local apprenticeship and training committee that he or she has the ability and aptitude to master the trade and also has enough education to complete satisfactorily the required instruction. The applicant must be physically capable of performing the work of the trade.

A local committee may establish additional qualifications as it deems necessary, but, according to the national standards, "such qualifications must be specific, clearly stated, and directly related to job performance."

In North America, the United Brotherhood of Carpenters and Joiners of America as well as the management groups that work with the union state firmly and clearly that selection of apprentices will be on the basis of qualifications alone—without regard to race, creed, color, or national origin: "All applicants shall be selected on the basis of objective standards and tests provided by the National Joint Carpentry Apprenticeship and Training Committee, which permit review after full and fair opportunity for application; and such program shall be operated on a completely nondiscriminatory basis."

Applying for Apprenticeship

If you live in a larger city, you can probably find a carpenters' joint-apprenticeship training program. Start at the United Brotherhood of Carpenters and Joiners' website (www.carpenters.org/common/locals.html) to get in touch with a union in your state or province. You can also consult your telephone book (check under "carpenter," "local," or "union" in the business white pages); direct inquiries to local contractors; or contact a field office of the U.S. Bureau of Apprenticeship and Training, or in Canada a provincial office of the Red Seal program. Refer to Appendix B at the back of the book for a list of these offices. In addition, an office of the state employment service might be a source of information and assistance in the United States.

Because of limited facilities and personnel, some apprenticeship training schools cannot accept all applicants as quickly as they would like. Class enrollments are limited. After fourth-year apprentices have completed their work and received their journeyman certificates, each successive class moves up, and this creates openings for first-year apprentices.

At least thirty days' public notice is given in advance of the earliest date for application for admission to the program. Joint training committees must accept applications over a period of not fewer than two weeks. All applicants who are placed on a list of eligible candidates will be retained on the list, subject to selection, for a period of two years.

In some areas, training directors ask applicants to present letters of recommendation from two former employers (if you have two), letters of character reference (usually two), a birth certificate, a training certificate or high school diploma (if you have one), and a military discharge (if applicable).

After your application is checked by officers of the apprenticeship training program, a letter will be sent either to you or to your high school to obtain a transcript of your grades. Upon receiving this request, the high school will mail the transcript directly to the apprenticeship training office.

Aptitude tests are given periodically by many training committees, and you will be notified when you can take such a test. The test is designed to show your language and reading ability, your ability with arithmetic used in the trade, and your natural talent for carpentry. Later, you'll be notified by mail whether you passed or failed the test.

An informal interview is arranged by some joint committees to give you full details of the program, inform you of the wages you'll receive during apprenticeship, and offer you other special information. You will be invited to ask any questions you may have during this interview.

If you meet all of the qualifications, you're ready for the first stage of apprenticeship training.

Getting into the Apprenticeship Program

A major consideration in getting into a carpentry apprenticeship program is your ability to be placed in on-the-job training. If, by chance, you are able to obtain ahead of time from an employer an *intent to hire*—a statement that will show a local joint committee or training school that a contractor is prepared to hire you as an apprentice—then you have taken a major step toward entering a carpentry apprenticeship.

If, however, you go first to the training school or committee and you pass the preliminary requirements, the school or local union may provide you with a letter of introduction and a list of potential employers. If one of these contractors agrees to hire you as an apprentice, you would then return to the union and make appropriate arrangements for work-study.

Term of Apprenticeship

The normal term of apprenticeship for the carpentry trade is four calendar years (between 5,200 and 8,000 work hours), consisting of eight six-month periods of reasonably continuous employment, including the probationary period and the required hours of supplemental school instruction. (Note: Working a forty-hour week for fifty-two weeks a year would total 2,080 hours of work and training per year; hence, the 5,200- to 8,000-hour total required. Because of employment uncertainties, training groups are lenient as to total time served.) For a three-year specialty program, the minimum number of hours is 3,900.

The local or areawide Joint Apprenticeship and Training Committee may, through the reevaluation process, accelerate the advancement of an apprentice who shows ability and mastery of the trade to the level for which he or she is qualified. On the other hand, the standard term of apprenticeship may be extended by the local or areawide committee for one year upon satisfactory proof that the apprentice cannot command the minimum scale of wages paid to journeymen.

Apprentice applicants who have had previous creditable training and are experienced in the trade or who have had some related instruction may be granted advanced standing on the basis of demonstrated ability and knowledge. If the local committee grants advanced standing, the apprentice shall be paid the rate of the period to which he or she is advanced.

An apprentice agreement is drawn up between the trainee and the trainer or training organization. If you are seventeen, a parent or guardian will be expected to sign your trainee agreement. The document is a protection for you, in that it assures you of training and preparation for a career as long as you live up to the standards required. It is also a protection for the committee or the employer, because it assures them that you will keep your part of the training bargain.

Apprentices employed under these standards are subject to a tryout or probationary period that should not exceed ninety days of "reasonably continuous employment." This period is designed as a final check on the trainee's fitness for the work.

During any probationary period, annulment of the apprentice agreement may be made by the local joint committee upon written request of any party (including you) for due cause, such as lack of progress or lack of interest.

If, for any reason, you are forced to drop out of an apprentice training program and you reenter it later, you will be given full credit for time served. All claims of previous experience will be evaluated, and you will be paid the wage rate for the training in which you are classified.

On-the-Job Training

When you start as an apprentice on the job, you will be given a variety of tasks at construction projects. These varied assignments give you the work experience required to cover the wide range of job functions you'll need to know.

Pay for on-the-job work comes from the contractor on the project. Pay scales are based upon the collective bargaining agreement between the union and the area contractors.

Like others in the building trades, carpenters expect loss of work time once a project is completed and from seasonal dips in work volume. These work fluctuations apply to the apprentice, also. However, competent workers are so valued that work is usually available to them at other job sites.

Putting in the Hours

The schedules shown in Table 7.1 are examples of the types of work experience and training considered necessary to develop skilled and productive workers in the carpentry trades. Within the limits of basic trade requirements, the schedule is adaptable to local conditions.

Table 7.1 Training and Hours Needed in the Carpentry Trades

Category	Approximate Hours
Carpenter	
General knowledge	325–500
Concrete formwork	975–1,500
Wood framing	975–1,500
Metal framing	650–1,000
Exterior finish	650–1,000
Interior finish	650–1,000
Supplemental skills	975–1,500
Total	5,200–8,000
Residential Carpenter	
General knowledge	280–375
Concrete formwork	730–1,125
Wood framing	730–1,125
Metal framing	477–750
Exterior finish	477–750
Interior finish	476–750
Supplemental skills	730–6,000
Total	3,900–6,000
Millwright	
General knowledge	325–500
Machine components	1,300–2,000
Machinery installation	1,300–2,000
Machinery alignment	1,300–2,000
Supplemental skills	975–1,500
Total	5,200–8,000
Cabinetmaker	
General knowledge	325–500
Machining	1,430–2,200
Assembly	1,625–2,500
Surface preparation and finish	650–1,000
Installation	975–1,500
Supplemental skills	195–300
Total	5,200–8,000

Work Experience for Other Specialties

Related to carpentry is the skilled work of the men and women who install ceiling systems and the various modern interior systems. In the 1980s some technical schools and apprenticeship training programs sought to establish separate tracks for students in the installation of curtain walls, suspended ceilings, pedestal floors (flooring suspended above a base floor to allow computer cables and other electrical conduits underneath), and other innovations of interior designers and architects. They awarded journeyman certificates to students who completed four thousand hours of work in these areas. It soon became evident, however, that these interior systems installers still needed the basic skills of carpentry to do their jobs well. Because of this, training leaders began integrating interior systems skills into the basic carpentry work experience on an elective basis.

There is also the work experience needed to become journeyman pile drivers. As with other disciplines, they must receive related classroom instructions to qualify them for all types of work in their particular fields. Pile driver trainees get instruction in accident prevention, first aid, safety hazards, and state and federal safety codes. The construction of cofferdam excavations and shoring excavations and the floating of water drivers are explained. In addition, the pile driver must know something about bridge construction, overpasses, underpasses, and dock building. (See schedules in Table 7.2.)

There are a growing number of specialty contractors in the construction industry. To supply skilled workers for such contractors, carpentry instructors have established a more flexible curriculum. These expanded work schedules, which were introduced in the 1990s, are similar to the curricula college students use in picking their major subjects of study and their electives. For example, an

Table 7.2 Training and Hours Needed in Carpentry-Related Trades

Category	Approximate Hours
Interior Systems Carpenter	
General knowledge	325–500
Framing	1,300–2,000
Wall systems	1,300–2,000
Ceiling systems	1,300–2,000
Supplemental systems	975–1,500
Total	5,200–8,000
Floor Layer	
General knowledge	350–500
Preparation	975–1,500
Materials	650–1,000
Layout and installation	1,625–2,500
Projects	950–1,500
Supplemental skills	650–1,000
Total	5,200–8,000
Drywall Applicator Specialist	
General knowledge	325–500
Framing	650–1,000
Wall systems	975–1,500
Ceiling systems	975–1,500
Supplemental skills	975–1,500
Total	3,900–6,000
Acoustical Carpenter Specialist	
General knowledge	325–500
Framing	975–1,500
Ceiling systems	1,625–2,500
Supplemental skills	975–1,500
Total	3,900–6,000
Lathing Specialist	
General knowledge	325–500
Framing	975–1,500
Ceiling systems	1,625–2,500
Supplemental skills	975–1,500
Total	3,900–6,000

(continued)

Table 7.2 Training and Hours Needed in Carpentry-Related Trades (continued)

Category	Approximate Hours
Pile Driver	
General knowledge	325–500
Concrete formwork	1,300–2,000
Pile installation	975–1,500
Foundation, shoring, and underpinning systems	975–1,500
Metal	975–1,500
Supplemental skills	650–1,000
Total	5,200–8,000

apprentice working for an interior systems contractor might be required to train in the areas of interior finish, interior systems, lathing, comprehensive skills, and knowledge (such as safety and first aid; the use of the transit, level, and laser; and the installation of scaffolding). Such electives might be the trainee's major focus of training.

In the interior systems specialty, as in others, the apprentice must remain in his or her specialty area of study until at least 80 percent of the skills and tasks listed by the school in that particular area are accomplished.

The apprentice might elect to complete his or her training in the area of hardwood flooring or exterior finish because of the need for such skills in shopping malls, restaurants, and other commercial structures that call for special interior effects and decor.

The system of majors and electives not only provides workers for modern construction technologies, but it produces more employable apprentices and journeymen. In addition to the interior systems specialty, there are other specialized trade skills that offer career opportunities to carpentry trainees.

One area of specialty contracting is that whereby carpenters work full-time creating and installing exhibits and displays for trade shows. Every major city and resort area has hotels and exhibition halls where exhibits are installed for convention delegates and trade show visitors. Special skills are needed for assembling and installing the components of an exhibit. Many exhibit components are patented and require detailed instructions for assembly. There are pipes and frameworks to be put together and drapes and decorations to be installed. Most exhibits require special shipping crates to be built. After a show is over, displays must be dismantled and shipped to new locations.

Among other specialties that carpentry apprentices may pursue at some training schools are cabinet manufacturing and fixture work. These are in addition to the basic training of cabinetmaking.

At the end of this chapter, you will find an explanation of the Performance Evaluated Training System, or PETS, which was developed by the United Brotherhood of Carpenters and Joiners of America and incorporated in the National Apprenticeship and Training Standards for carpentry. The PETS program has so-called "skill-blocks" for trainees in the work experience specialties.

In the Classroom

While the apprentice is undergoing on-the-job training, he or she is also devoting time to classroom study. In some cities, such instruction is highly organized with well-equipped classrooms and highly skilled instructors. The apprentice who is in a training program thus equipped is fortunate and should have no difficulty putting in the required hours of classroom instruction (approximately 144 hours per year for each of the four years of apprenticeship).

In many major cities, including Philadelphia, New York, and Chicago, training leaders work closely with public school officials and are permitted to use public educational facilities for classroom instruction. In Philadelphia, for example, the board of education provides the instructors as well as classroom space at the Mastbaum Vocational-Technical Annex.

Experience has shown that the best school instructors are those who have worked at the trade. The United Brotherhood of Carpenters and Joiners of America holds periodic seminars for instructors to brief them on the latest developments in the trade and on proper training methods. Some training programs are operated in conjunction with private or publicly operated trade schools. In such cases, instructors must meet the accepted standards of the trade. Under no circumstances can the hours of work and hours of school exceed the maximum number of hours prescribed by state, provincial, or federal law for a person of the age of the apprentice.

At the close of each six-month period of study and training, the apprentices in some areas must pass an examination in order to advance to the next period. When they pass the last of these examinations, they receive a completion certificate stating that they have successfully completed their training and are qualified to work as carpenters, cabinetmakers, or millwrights, depending upon their particular course of work.

Carpentry Training in Canada

Training in carpentry and other skilled trades through apprenticeship has much support in the provinces of Canada. Many early immigrants to Canada were from France, Scotland, Germany, Poland, and other European nations, where training in the skilled trades is a way of life for young people. Many community colleges, such as Academy Canada (www.academycanada.com), offer vocational training in carpentry. Local unions and councils of the United Brotherhood of Carpenters and Joiners of America offer apprenticeship training under the same basic plan as their counterparts in the United States.

To qualify for labor-management training in Canada, a person needs at least a tenth-grade education or proof of equivalency. Schools in Ontario and some other provinces offer preapprenticeship training, the funds for which are supplied by the provincial government. There are also training school openings for minorities, who sometimes face unwelcoming work environments as a result of carpenters who perceive them as threats. The Carpenters Local 27 Training Centre in Toronto makes a special effort to reach out to women and minorities, and both groups account for a significant portion of the trainees there.

The Performance Evaluated Training System (PETS)

PETS is basically a method of teaching certain job processes by means of a step-by-step visual presentation. The Carpenters Union developed the pioneering method of teaching apprentices in the late 1970s. The PETS training method enables apprentices to progress in their education at their own pace. They can study the audiovisual presentation, perform the task described, and, if they and their instructors are not satisfied that they have performed the task well, the apprentices can perform it again and again, following the visuals until they get it right. PETS training materials for millwrights include audio instruction with the visuals.

Under this system, the instructor becomes a resource person who is ready to answer questions and offer advice, but much is left up to the PETS equipment to provide the instruction.

The particular trade—carpentry, millwright, cabinetmaking, or floor laying—is divided into various teaching sections. Each of these sections is then further divided into skill blocks. Each block covers the necessary blueprint reading, safety factors, and tool skills necessary for that particular job process.

Advancement under the PETS system is based upon completion of specific numbers of skill blocks. The completion of six blocks entitles an apprentice to advancement in educational position and usually brings advancement in pay. Early completion of the blocks required in a given year does not release the apprentice from the obligation of attending school for the required number of hours that year, but it does indicate he or she is ready to move ahead, once the time has elapsed.

8

THE TRAINING PERIOD

THE APPLICANT WHO is accepted for apprenticeship is issued a probationary identification card. Upon completion of the probationary period and on being admitted to the union and properly indentured—that is, officially contracted as an apprentice—he or she is issued a regular work card. Under United States standards, the probationary period is not to exceed ninety days of reasonably continuous employment. In most training programs, the joint committee furnishes apprentices with periodic report cards, which are filled in by the apprentices and forwarded to the secretary of the committee at the end of each period. Unless this report is sent in, no credit for work accomplished will be given. The evaluations usually come at six-month intervals.

The joint labor-management training committee keeps a master record of all apprentice work experience and related instruction. In some cities, the training schools forward testing results and other records directly to the joint committee.

The training committee has certain responsibilities during the apprentice's training period. It must see to it that the apprentice works with a competent journeyman and that he or she is provided, as much as possible, with continuous employment. If it is impossible for one employer to provide the different types of craft experience necessary to give the apprentice all-around carpentry training, or if the employer's business is of such a character as not to permit reasonably continuous employment over the entire period of apprenticeship, the local joint committee may arrange to transfer the apprentice to another employer, who will assume all the terms and conditions of the local standards. However, no apprentice will be transferred to an employer who has not signed an apprentice agreement.

In Canada, apprenticeship is a three-way partnership involving the apprentice, the employer, and the government. Specifics vary from province to province, but the Canadian Council of Directors of Apprenticeship oversees interprovincial standards as part of the Red Seal program. The provincial governments set tuition fees for classroom work, maintain records on apprentices and journeymen, and supervise examinations during apprenticeships. In some cases, they may also provide funds for apprentices to acquire the necessary tools.

Work and Training Standards

If either the apprentice or the employer becomes dissatisfied with the other's performance, each party has the right and privilege of appealing to the local joint apprenticeship committee for action or adjustment in an effort to remedy the situation. The decision of the committee is final in all matters not in conflict with approved local agreements and with apprenticeship training standards.

The apprentice is to be paid on a "progressive percentage of the journeyman's wage rate, preferably at six-month intervals, and average not less than approximately 70 to 75 percent of the journeyman's rate over the apprenticeship term." These are standards established by the U.S. Department of Labor. During the training period, the apprentice is to expect these wage levels and no more. The Canadian provinces and territories have similar wage scales determined by government trade regulations, agreements made with unions, or both. See Appendix B for listings of U.S. and Canadian apprenticeship offices.

The hours of work and the working conditions for an apprentice are the same as those covering journeymen. This applies to overtime work as well as regular work. However, under recommended standards, no apprentice shall be allowed to work overtime if it interferes with his or her related school instruction. Apprentices who are absent from work through their own fault are rightfully expected to make up such lost time before advancing to the next period of apprenticeship.

The National Apprenticeship and Training Committee urges all local joint apprenticeship and training committees to include in their training standards a provision stating that, in addition to the progressive wage percentage, apprentices are eligible for and shall receive the same fringe benefits provided journeymen under the local labor-management bargaining agreement. It also recommends that wages and benefits be combined when establishing wage determinations for a given area.

Safety Standards

Construction sites typically experience a relatively high incidence of accidents. Many men and women from the various trades are working together on these sites, and often their jobs cross paths. There is a daily accumulation of debris, and workers have to watch their step, lest they trip over something or slip on spilled water, oils, or chemicals.

The necessity of working on temporary platforms and stages, plus individual carelessness, adds to the carpenter's hazards. Often, in major construction, carpenters must work high above the ground, and therefore they must always carefully follow the safety rules of the job.

On most jobs, a hard hat of strong, reinforced plastic and a sturdy head liner is required, as are hard shoes with built-in reinforcements against heavy objects being dropped on toes and feet.

Safe work habits are stressed throughout the apprentice training period. Apprentices will learn that horseplay is strictly forbidden in most work situations.

The National Safety Council, the union, and the contractors have safety manuals for training purposes. Some of these manuals are used in classroom instruction. In addition, alert employers display posters and warning signs at the job site and enforce established safety regulations.

In 1968, building and construction trade unions played a major role in the enactment of improved federal construction safety laws, which call for the full compliance of the industry with federal and state safety inspections. The apprentice, as well as the journeyman, has a responsibility to call the employer's and fellow worker's attention to hazards on the job.

The National Apprenticeship and Training Standards state:

> The employer shall instruct the apprentice in safe and healthful work practices and shall ensure that the apprentice is trained in facilities and other environments that are in compliance with

either the occupational safety and health standards promulgated by the Secretary of Labor under Public Law 91-596, dated December 29, 1970, or state standards that have been found to be at least as effective.

Additional Standards

Recognized apprenticeship training programs in America are governed by standards drawn up by a National Joint Carpentry Apprenticeship and Training Committee representing the United Brotherhood of Carpenters and Joiners of America, Associated General Contractors of America, and the National Association of Home Builders. The committee works in conjunction with the Bureau of Apprenticeship and Training of the U.S. Department of Labor in preparing the national standards. The up-to-date standards are periodically printed by the United States Government Printing Office in Washington, DC, for distribution to joint apprenticeship and training committees, coordinators, and other leaders of the program. In Canada, standards come from provincial governments with input from industry and the federal government.

The tradition of training according to these standards is the result of many years of work and refinement by people in the field, and it represents some of the most respected training programs in any trade discipline today.

9

ALTERNATIVE PATHS

IN AN EFFORT to reduce unemployment among young people, the federal government has appropriated funds through various agencies for job training in recent years. In the 1960s, one of the ways it conducted President Lyndon Johnson's War on Poverty was by training young men and women under the Manpower Development and Training Administration (MDTA). Another avenue was the Job Corps, which was established in 1964. In the mid-1970s, MDTA became CETA—the Comprehensive Employment and Training Administration. And in 1982, Congress enacted the Job Training Partnership Act (JTPA) to replace CETA. In the 1990s, the JTPA, together with the Job Corps, represented the major federal funding efforts to train young people for jobs.

Finally, in 2000, after Congress made more changes in manpower training, the Workforce Investment Act replaced the JTPA, expanded the Job Corps program, and consolidated the work of related agencies.

Job Corps

Job Corps is a no-cost educational and vocational training program administered by the U.S. Department of Labor that helps young people ages sixteen through twenty-four get better jobs, make more money, and take control of their lives. Students enroll to learn a trade, earn a high school diploma or GED, and get help finding a good job in such trades as automotive repair, forestry, cement masonry, painting, heavy-equipment operations, and, of course, carpentry.

Preapprenticeship training in carpentry is a big part of Job Corps activity at many of its training centers. Participants usually live at a Job Corps training center and receive a monthly allowance upon joining the program; the longer they stay, the larger their allowance becomes. (All Job Corps members receive a monthly stipend ranging from $100 to $150. Job Corps offers a one-time $250 payment for getting a job within six months of completing the program, another $100 for getting a job in the field studied, $250 for students who earn a diploma or GED while in the program, and a bonus for completing the program.) Meanwhile, they are provided with room and board in barracks and mess halls. Job Corps provides career counseling and transition support to its students for up to twelve months after they graduate from the program.

Job Corps recruits trainees through referrals from various public and private agencies. Joint labor-management apprenticeship committees maintained by unions and contractors refer trainees, as do state employment offices. You may apply directly by calling Job Corps at (800) 733-JOBS and requesting an enrollment packet. You can locate a training center near you by calling the same number or visiting http://jobcorps.doleta.gov/jcportal.cfm. Candidates for the Job Corps are screened for aptitude and evaluated at various Job Corps training centers. The evaluation panel usually consists of the center director, the educational director, and the coordinator. Potential Job Corps members must have sincere interest in becoming carpenters, painters, or craftspersons in one of the many skills taught. They must demonstrate an ability to perform simple mechanical operations and meet other general selection criteria.

There are eighty-two Job Corps centers around the United States offering training in carpentry. Funding for the centers comes variously from the Department of Labor and also from the Departments of Agriculture and the Interior. Instructors and training materials are supplied by the Carpenters Union and by private industry, with the help of federal funds. Upon acceptance into the Job Corps, students undergo one to two years of instruction. In carpentry, instruction is generally a year. Some of the training is in classrooms and leads to the equivalent of a high school diploma, but equal emphasis is placed on job skills.

The job skills training is a combination of craft-related instruction and on-the-job experience. Trainees engage in the construction of real buildings and other structures. They perform all of the work normally done by journeyman carpenters, learning to use a transit and level to lay out buildings, using basic tools for the rough framing, and doing interior and exterior finishing and trim. Many of the building projects are for public use on or near the centers. These skills are intended to give Job Corps members the aptitude they need to qualify as a carpenter apprentice (or other skilled labor trainee) at the end of their training.

When the Job Corps was launched in the 1960s, some training centers were established in cities, where the trainees were readily available. The Office of Economic Opportunity found, however, that it was best to place Job Corps members in rural and even wilderness locations, where plenty of space was available, there were few distractions, and projects could be undertaken that would be of value to the public. For example, Job Corps members build shelters and wayside cabins in the national parks and make repairs to existing facilities in state and federal forest preserves.

Job Corps programs require a concerted effort, but their overall track record has shown success. Within one year of graduation from the program (or for former enrollees, within ninety days of exit), 84 percent of Job Corps participants got jobs or enrolled in further training. Sixty-four percent earned a high school diploma or GED while in the program.

The Carpenters Union—the United Brotherhood of Carpenters and Joiners of America—encourages sincere applicants for apprenticeship training in the United States who do not qualify for such training to seriously consider the Job Corps route. If, after counseling with the joint apprenticeship and training committee, the students agree, they are given referral cards and directed to a local Job Corps screener. If they meet the Job Corps criteria for entry, they're assigned to a Job Corps Center near their home. After a student completes one year's training, he or she may then apply for direct entry into the apprenticeship program.

The Carpenters Union has been very successful in placing Job Corps graduates into various apprenticeship training programs. Since it became involved in the program almost a quarter of a century ago, Job Corps has accepted several thousand young men and women for apprenticeship training, and many of these apprentices have gone on to become full-fledged journeymen carpenters. Others were accepted in millcabinet shops, in modular or prefabrication plants, or in other areas of the industry. Some have even decided to become Job Corps instructors.

SkillsUSA

SkillsUSA assists high school and college-age students with training to enter trade, technical, and skilled service occupations, including carpentry. SkillsUSA is a nonprofit group, originally founded as the Vocational Industrial Clubs of America (VICA) in 1965, and it serves more than 284,000 members through 14,700 sections in fifty-four states and territories. Each career group has its own division within the organization, and each operates at the local, state, and national levels. Students form clubs at their schools within their own occupational area, with the help of their instructors. The activity is included as part of the school curriculum. SkillsUSA has assisted 8.8 million members in its forty-plus-year history.

Working with vocational instructors and other school leaders, SkillsUSA trains young people in leadership skills and shows them how to apply special craft skills, such as carpentry and cabinet-making, toward achieving a livelihood after their school days are over. The organization holds local, state, and national competitions in eighty-four occupational and leadership skill areas, including carpentry and other crafts and trades; and it holds regular club meetings, publishes a national magazine, and participates in international vocational club programs. The U.S. Department of Education has called the organization a "successful model of [an] employer-driven youth development training program." For more information, visit www.skillsusa.org.

Skills Canada

Skills Canada, which is the Canadian counterpart to SkillsUSA, has expanded to serve all of the country's provinces and territories.

Its mission is "to champion and stimulate the development of excellent technological and leadership skills in Canadian youth." Like its American counterpart, Skills Canada has provincial skills competitions for aspiring carpenters, cabinetmakers, and other craft workers that culminate in an annual national competition. The program also sends its winners to the biennial WorldSkills competition (www.worldskills.org). For more information about Skills Canada, visit www.skillscanada.com.

Less-Traveled Roads to Training

The U.S. Department of Veterans Affairs also offers advice and counsel to military veterans organizations, advising them on how veterans may obtain special vocational training. Veterans are advised to check with the Department of Veterans Affairs and local veterans organizations as to the availability of any local programs in carpentry and allied skills.

Army Reserves and the regular military offer a limited amount of training in the skilled trades, such as carpentry. In forty hours of "core training," many army reservists learn how to use electrical and pneumatic tools as well as how to do plumbing and surveying work. They then have an option of taking either forty additional hours of carpentry and blueprint reading or an equal number of hours in electrical wiring and welding.

One way to learn the basics of carpentry is by enrolling in a correspondence course. Such training is offered by Penn Foster, an international correspondence school that has served thirteen million students in its more than one hundred years in business. To learn more about Penn Foster's carpentry program, visit www.penn foster.edu/carpenter/index.html. Note that these are for-profit programs. Also, keep in mind that any correspondence training in carpentry should be accompanied by hands-on experience.

Carpentry and cabinetmaking are two skills that are much in demand in the Peace Corps. For those adventurous individuals who would like to become vocational teachers themselves, carpentry becomes an asset for serving the developing nations of the world through the Peace Corps' Education, Youth Outreach, and Community Development branch. For more information, you can visit www.peacecorps.org.

10

Professional Organizations

THE ONLY WORKER organization devoted exclusively to the craft of carpentry is the United Brotherhood of Carpenters and Joiners of America, a trade union founded in 1881. It has headquarters in Washington, DC, on Constitution Avenue, just below Capitol Hill. The United Brotherhood of Carpenters and Joiners of America represents more than half a million carpenters, cabinetmakers, millwrights, and other skilled workers in the United States and Canada.

Early Craft Guilds

In the year 1333, in London, England, a group of carpenters founded their own labor organization. They called it the Carpenters' Guild of London, and it still exists as one of the oldest social institutions in Great Britain.

The guild required members to attend mass in midwinter and to pay dues amounting to one penny per person. The ordinances also provided for attendance at funerals of deceased members and made provision for the guild to pay for the services of its poor members. Sick members and those out of work were given assistance.

The Carpenters' Guild of London received a formal charter from the Crown in 1477, and a coat-of-arms was produced. In time, the guilds came to be called companies, and it was as companies that the first carpenter organizations were formed in America.

It was in historic old Carpenters' Hall in Philadelphia, Pennsylvania, that the First Continental Congress of the American Colonies met in 1774. Carpenters' Hall had been built to house the Carpenters' Company of the city, a guildlike group of carpenters whose work ornamented the city. Carpenters in the colonies were master builders. They acted as architects, contractors, and wood craftsmen, advising gentlemen such as Benjamin Franklin and Thomas Jefferson on the practicality of their construction ideas.

Early carpenters unions scored several "firsts" in the trade union movement of North America. They were the first to establish as a trade principle a "book of prices" for accepting pay for their work "so that a workman should receive the worth of his money." Philadelphia carpenters were also the first to strike for a ten-hour workday. That was in 1791. A century later they led the American labor movement's drive for an eight-hour workday.

The carpenters' unions have come forward in times of war and performed heroic service in the construction of army camps and installations and in providing housing for displaced persons.

The present-day organization of carpenters—the United Brotherhood of Carpenters and Joiners of America—was formed in a small union hall in Chicago, Illinois, on August 12, 1881. This date appears on the official seal of the union today. The union is one of the oldest in the American labor movement. Its first meeting did not get much attention in the newspapers of the day. The *Chicago Tribune* noted that "the Knights of the Bench and Sawbuck" were meeting at 192 Washington Street. Much of their time was spent developing a constitution.

Originally, there were thirty-six delegates from fourteen local unions in eleven cities, representing 2,042 carpenters. They came from Cleveland; Indianapolis; Kansas City; Philadelphia; Buffalo; Detroit; New York City; Washington, DC; St. Louis; Cincinnati; and Chicago—a good representation of America's growing cities at the time.

In those days a carpenter worked for two dollars a day. The average workday was ten hours, and the average workweek was six days. The young union suffered the tribulations of all labor unions in those days—few members, little funds, and difficulties in organizing. Labor unions had few of the legal protections that they enjoy today. Workers could be locked out without cause and were often forced to sign "yellow dog" contracts stating that they would not join a union. Hours were long and working conditions were often dangerous.

In 1886, when the American Federation of Labor (AFL) was formed, the carpenters were well represented with a delegation at the founding convention. Two of the top officers of the AFL were carpenters: Peter J. McGuire, first secretary of the United Brotherhood of Carpenters and Joiners and the man generally credited with establishing Labor Day, and Gabriel Edmonston, first president of the Carpenters Union.

Today its headquarters is an imposing five-story structure at the foot of Capitol Hill in Washington, DC, where Brotherhood leaders, researchers, statisticians, attorneys, and educators direct and coordinate the work of this broad organization. The Brotherhood severed its relationship with the AFL-CIO in 2001 and for a time formed a temporary alliance with the Change to Win Coalition and the New Unity Partnership, which has since ended. The Carpenters Union is essentially a craft union, as distinguished from an industrial union. This means that the union is made up mainly of members of a particular trade or craft.

Any carpenters, cabinetmakers, or millwrights employed in a large industrial plant are enlisted as members of a craft union. This craft union is separate from the industrial unions in the plant, which are primarily organized to represent the unskilled workers. In industrial relations jargon, it is said that the carpenters "carve out a craft unit" in the plant. The principal advantage to the skilled workers enlisted as members of a craft unit is that they maintain their wage and benefits level above that of the unskilled workers.

There are instances, however, where the Carpenters Union has organized plants on an industrial basis, enlisting every worker eligible for union membership, regardless of his or her skill. This is done primarily to give the advantages of union representation to workers who might otherwise not be covered by a union contract. Union carpenters, for example, have organized pleasure-boat factories, prefabrication plants, and so on.

Each local union elects local officers, draws up bylaws, and usually elects (funds permitting) one or more business agents. The agents' responsibilities are to deal with management on a day-to-day basis, assign union members to jobs, locate work for them, and operate the union hall.

To be eligible for the benefits of union membership, a member must be in good standing, with dues paid. Dues books or dues cards are carried on the person to indicate membership in good standing.

Management Organizations

The primary management groups in the field are the Associated General Contractors of America (AGC), the National Association of Home Builders, and the Associated Builders and Contractors, Incorporated, all of which maintain headquarters in or near the nation's capital. Of the three, the AGC is the largest and strongest.

The AGC (www.agc.org), as the only national organization of general contractors embracing all types of construction, has as its primary purposes "to represent and serve as the spokesman for the general contracting industry; to seek to improve construction methods, management and service; to eliminate uneconomical and improper practices; and to build skill, integrity, and responsibility throughout the industry." As a national organization with more than thirty-three thousand members in a hundred chapters and branches throughout the United States, the AGC serves both the national and local needs of general contractors.

As its name suggests, the National Association of Home Builders (www.nahb.org) is concerned with residential construction. It has branches and offices throughout the country and is concerned with building codes, the technology of the industry, federal activities in home construction, and so on.

The union and the two management groups described above participate jointly in an international apprenticeship training program. In addition, each independently supports various vocational training activities, including those funded under the Department of Labor's Employment and Training Administration.

The third major organization in the field is the Associated Builders and Contractors (www.abc.org), which has its headquarters in Arlington, Virginia, as well as seventy-nine chapters throughout the United States. This management association is made up primarily of "open shop" or what ABC calls "merit shop" contractors and builders, which means that its members are opposed to "closed shop" or "union shop" conditions among their building tradespeople.

There are also contractors and builders in the construction industry that employ both union work crews and nonunion work crews. ABC supports the Trimmer Education Foundation, a nonprofit organization established in 1971 by a group of ABC builders and contractors "to sponsor research and education to improve the technology and environment of the construction industry."

There are also many specialized management groups in the industry: the NEA—the Association of Union Constructors (www.nea-online.org); the Association of the Wall and Ceiling Industry (www.awci.org); the Association of Crane and Rigging Professionals (www.acrp.net); the Building Trades Association (www.buildingtrades.com); and others. All are organized as trade associations to improve industry conditions and to deal with government regulations.

In Canada, the Canadian Construction Association (www.cca-acc.com/home.html) represents the broad concerns of the construction industry nationally with an eye toward business owners and leaders. Among its aims are to "develop and promote approved standard tendering and contractual practices and procedures with the design professions and with owners" and to "promote harmonious working relationships among its members for the benefit of the industry as a whole."

The Canadian Homebuilders' Association (www.chba.ca) covers the residential side, advocating only for builders and renovators, particularly on the effects of government regulations and standards. See Appendix C for an abbreviated list of trade associations.

11

Moving Up

EXPERIENCE IN THE building and construction industry has shown that the best contractors and supervisors are men and women who have served as journeymen in the industry. Carpenters who have worked at all stages of a construction project—from the foundation work to the finishing touches at completion—are often ideally suited to move into managerial positions. Many go into business for themselves as private contractors.

The young man or woman who wants to go far in the industry might wish to take advantage of postgraduate studies through journeyman training classes or courses in junior or technical colleges.

Advancement Possibilities

The following are some of the jobs open to the journeyman who has ambition:

- **Foreman.** Supervises all journeymen of his or her particular trade on a project. Plans work, maintains schedules, and works under the job superintendent.
- **Job superintendent.** Directs all construction functions on small or medium-sized projects or on specific phases of major projects. Directs work crews through their foremen.
- **General superintendent.** Carries out directions of the project manager, job superintendents, and subcontractors.
- **Project manager.** Directs all construction functions on large projects, coordinating the work of all units. He or she also establishes schedules, working procedures, and job policies.
- **Estimator.** Obtains basic data concerning a proposed construction project, usually from plans and specifications. These data include quantities of materials, the number of hours necessary to perform certain types of work, methods to be used, and equipment required. With the assistance of other members of the contractor's office staff, he or she then computes the cost of construction, which represents the contractor's competitive bid for the job.
- **Expeditor.** Maintains construction schedules by reviewing deliveries, scheduling the arrival of materials and workers at job sites, establishing priorities, and obtaining clearances.
- **Purchasing agent.** Determines the most economical source of materials; stores supplies, equipment, and parts; and ensures the lowest price consistent with delivery schedules.
- **Office manager.** Maintains an office to centralize supervisory work on the construction site. He or she keeps records, bills clients, makes up payrolls, and handles mail.
- **Engineer.** Takes soil and material samples, tests, plans, surveys, and in other ways researches and offers professional recommendations to the contractor as to the best building procedures.

Some journeyman carpenters have gone back to school and prepared themselves for jobs as construction engineers.

• **Architect.** Designs the buildings and draws up plans and specifications. Students of architecture in colleges often spend their summers working construction jobs to become familiar with building materials and construction techniques. An apprentice or journeyman carpenter who enjoys design work might consider advanced education in architecture.

Most of the jobs just mentioned apply to advancements from general carpentry. Millcabinet workers and millwrights can advance to foremen and job superintendents. Cabinetmakers might become shop managers and might even go into business for themselves. Millwrights have also gone into business for themselves, pulling together teams of skilled millwrights to bid on jobs.

Self-Employment

We often dream about being our own bosses and going into business for ourselves. It is possible to achieve this dream through carpentry and the allied trades, but the change from wage earner to a self-employed person requires careful financial preparation.

To become a contractor, a journeyman must be prepared to bid competitively with giants in the business and to suffer financial losses due to the seasonal and material-shortage nature of the industry. In many cases, contractors must be bonded against failure to complete the assigned work.

As in all business ventures, the qualities of hard work, good character, self-discipline, experience, and patience are prerequisites to success.

Many contractors got their start by knowing someone in the industry who had faith in their ability and advanced the necessary funds to get them started—or at least co-signed a note with them at a local bank. Bankers are experienced in dealing with building contractors and can offer sound financial advice to newcomers in the contracting business. Small contractors sometimes get started with a single successful bid for a job.

They should be prepared to follow up this initial success with bids on jobs of a similar size that they are able to complete on time.

One attractive option for carpenters in search of greater independence without the financial risk is signing on as an independent contractor with a franchised repair company. Such businesses can offer a good base of work on which to build while eliminating clerical and scheduling aspects and payment delays for jobs.

Many other journeymen have earned their livelihood through maintenance and repair work in industry and in the home. Such men and women list themselves in the yellow pages of telephone books and in classified advertisements. Their best advertising, however, is usually word-of-mouth reports of jobs well done from satisfied customers. Self-employed carpenters usually acquire their own trucks and maintain complete bins of hand tools and power tools to prepare themselves for any situation.

If you are planning to go into business for yourself, you would do well to study the successes of others, analyze the reasons for their success, and plot your future carefully and with determination. See Appendix A for resources for all manner of carpentry-related jobs.

12

The Carpenter of the Future

THE WORLD IS changing faster than ever before, and the construction and carpentry trades are not exempt from these advances. Carpenters who have been on the job for several years have already noticed numerous changes. Tools have become smaller, lighter, and more ergonomic. Cordless, battery-powered tools allow workers to roam a site freely and with less effort. Stronger, lighter composite framing materials offer structural support in some new buildings; innovative fasteners and adhesives form studier connections and bonds; and advanced soundproofing enhances quality of life. Many of these innovations make carpenters more efficient and competitive, and though that means fewer craftspersons can do more work, the advancements also fight downward pressure on wages stemming from immigration and a globalized economy. Openings for carpenters should still increase 10 to 15 percent over the next decade.

There are already clues to tomorrow's work style. Laser beams are used to survey job sites. With micrometer accuracy, a laser beam helps a millwright set an atomic reactor precisely. It also helps carpenters and pile drivers align pilings for docks. New building materials also are coming to the fore each succeeding decade, as chemists explore the new possibilities of raw materials. We have new laminations, new foam substances, new superhardeners, and many other innovations.

Planning: Urban, Suburban, Exurban

As North America changed from a predominantly rural society to a highly concentrated urban society in the twentieth century, carpenters found themselves working in planned communities, satellite cities, and residential cul-de-sacs. In the twenty-first century, there are few places carpenters won't work. Already some wandering souls are leaving the suburbs behind and forming new communities, known as exurbs, far from traditional cities of any kind. These residents might telecommute for work, or when necessary, they might connect with distant cities on the superhighways that take them where they need to go. Exurbs often pop up along existing interstate highways, however far they may be from major cities.

Others will choose to economize and, with energy supplies uncertain, live in established neighborhoods where mass transit is possible. We can expect to see a greater emphasis placed on mass transit in tomorrow's cities, and carpenters will be building subways, subway stations, perhaps even monorails as well as other systems for the mass movement of people. The older homes and historic buildings in the cores of cities will look to carpenters to keep them viable and attractive for years to come.

Science and Technology

Eventually, the spectacular things happening in the world of science and technology will undoubtedly change the work and the lifestyle of tomorrow's carpenter. Scientists are striving to improve life on earth through better shelters, climate controls, new ways of distributing food and clothing, and through newly developed communications systems.

They are plumbing the ocean depths for new ways to harvest the undersea world and for better methods of installing new structures under the waves. They are sending forth manned and unmanned spacecraft on missions of exploration that may eventually lead to space stations linking this planet with outposts elsewhere in the solar system. It is not far-fetched to imagine that many young people entering carpentry today will someday be in the vanguard of such fantastic developments.

Underwater Workers

Some carpenters and millwrights are employed on the offshore drilling platforms along our coasts. Occasionally, pile drivers have donned undersea gear for their work in some phase of dock construction. As scientists talk of year-round communities under the sea for the dredging of minerals and the developing and harvesting of fish, carpenters may be working in underwater airlocks. Researchers have already proven that it is feasible to live for periods of several weeks in underwater homes on the continental shelf.

Return to Space

Although the costs seem almost insurmountable today, there may be a time when human civilization will extend its realm to the moon and beyond—with solar stations, mining facilities, and research stations. Some wealthy industrialists already have plans to offer civilians the chance to fly on the edge of space for recreation. Richard Branson, head of the music company Virgin, is developing a Virgin Galactic spaceliner that could accommodate private citizens. Early rides might cost a cool $150,000. "If it is a success, we want to move into orbital flights and then, possibly, even get a hotel up there," Branson has told the BBC. And Amazon.com founder and CEO Jeff Bezos has moved ahead with plans for his space company, Blue Origin, to offer suborbital flights with precise takeoff and landing capabilities from his ranch in West Texas. In such cases, tomorrow's carpenters may wear spacesuits as they go about their work.

No Limits

We often hear executives publicly proclaiming the broadest possible missions for their companies. Automotive CEOs declare that they aren't in the car business; they're in the transportation business (or, depending on whom you ask, the toy business). Phone companies don't sell land lines or air time; they sell communications, convenience, or peace of mind. All these shifts in perspective are designed to prove the relevance of the companies involved. They don't want to limit their opportunities or lose market share by defining themselves too narrowly, as technological advancements and consumer preferences change how business gets done.

Carpenters have the luxury of not having to justify their existence or make grand forecasts about their capabilities. We know construction will be part of the future. At the same time, we must be careful not to restrict ourselves with traditional definitions of carpentry. Those entering the field today should be prepared to pick up new skills on the job and remain flexible as the scope of their work continues to expand.

Just as modern architectural designs have created demand for ceiling, wall, and flooring specialists, tomorrow's technologies will push us in new directions. Technological advancements, consumer needs, and international economics will drive us into new arenas— new working locations, building materials, tools, and structures. When they do, we must be prepared through our training and professional commitment to build the world to come, just as we've built this one.

Appendix A

Additional Resources

Publications

Books

Career Discovery Encyclopedia, 6th ed. Ferguson Publishing Co., 2006.

Career Guide to Industries (sections on construction, a companion to the *Occupational Outlook Handbook*). Compiled by the Bureau of Labor Statistics, U.S. Department of Labor. Published biennially; www.bls.gov/oco/cg/home.htm.

Career Information Center, 9th ed. Macmillan Reference Books, 2007.

Finish Carpentry (For Pros by Pros). From the editors of *Fine Homebuilding*. Taunton Press, 2003.

McKinney, Anne, ed. *Real-Résumés for Construction Jobs*. PREP Publishing, 2002.

Miller, Mark R., Rex Miller, and Glenn E. Baker. *Carpentry & Construction*, 4th ed. McGraw-Hill, 2004.

Occupational Outlook Handbook (sections on carpenters,
  millwrights, cabinetmakers; a large compendium on all
  classified occupations in the United States). Compiled by the
  Bureau of Labor Statistics, U.S. Department of Labor.
  Published biennially; www.bls.gov/oco/home.htm.
Simpson, Scot. *Framing & Rough Carpentry: The Illustrated Guide
  for Apprentices & Carpenters*, 2nd ed. (Builder's Essentials
  series). R.S. Means Company, 2001.

Periodicals

Carpenter
United Brotherhood of Carpenters and Joiners of America
101 Constitution Ave. NW
Washington, DC 20001
www.carpenters.org/carpentermag
Published quarterly

Constructor
Associated General Contractors of America
McGraw-Hill Construction Information Group
Two Penn Plaza, 9th Fl.
New York, NY 10121
www.constructor.construction.com
Published bimonthly

Engineering News-Record
McGraw-Hill Construction Information Group
Two Penn Plaza, 9th Fl.
New York, NY 10121
www.enr.com
Published weekly

The Journal of Light Construction
Hanley Wood, LLC
186 Allen Brook La.
Williston, VT 05495
www.jlconline.com
Published monthly

Tools of the Trade
Hanley Wood, LLC
One Thomas Circle NW, Ste. 600
Washington, DC 20005
www.toolsofthetrade.net
Published bimonthly

Wood & Wood Products
Vance Publications
P.O. Box 1400
Lincolnshire, IL 60069
www.iswonline.com/wwp
Published monthly

Websites

American Subcontractors Association
 www.asaonline.com
Bureau of Labor Statistics, U.S. Department of Labor
 www.bls.gov
Construction Jobs
 www.constructionjobs.com

Construction Safety Council
  www.buildsafe.org
GED Practice Tests
  www.testprepreview.com/ged_practice.htm
Job Corps
  http://jobcorps.doleta.gov
Monster
  http://hourlyandskilled.monster.com/trades/archives
National Association of Home Builders
  www.nahb.org
Peace Corps
  www.peacecorps.gov
Skills Canada
  www.skillscanada.com
SkillsUSA
  www.skillsusa.org
Small Business Administration
  www.sba.gov
Statistics Canada's Business Data
  http://commerce.statcan.ca/english/commerce
United Brotherhood of Carpenters and Joiners of America
  www.carpenters.org
  (Locate local unions through the "Local Contacts" link.)
U.S. Department of Veterans Affairs
  www.va.gov

Offices of Apprenticeship and Training

U.S. Bureau of Apprenticeship and Training, Regional Offices

The U.S. government maintains six regional offices of the U.S. Bureau of Apprenticeship, listed here with the states and territories they serve. Most states also have their own offices as well, and those addresses follow.

Region 1

Regional Director
USDOL/ETA/OATELS
JFK Federal Bldg., Rm. E-370
Boston, MA 02203
Griffin.John@dol.gov

Region 1 covers Connecticut, Maine, Massachusetts, New Hampshire, New Jersey, New York, Puerto Rico, Rhode Island, Vermont, and the Virgin Islands.

Region 2

Regional Director
USDOL/ETA/OATELS
Ste. 820-East 170 S. Independence Mall, West
Philadelphia, PA 19106
Hersh.Joseph@dol.gov

Region 2 covers Delaware, Maryland, Pennsylvania, Virginia, West Virginia, and the District of Columbia.

Region 3

Regional Director
USDOL/ETA/OATELS
61 Forsyth St. SW, Rm. 6T71
Atlanta, GA 30303
Garner.Garfield@dol.gov

Region 3 covers Alabama, Florida, Georgia, Kentucky, Mississippi, North Carolina, South Carolina, and Tennessee.

Region 4

Regional Director
USDOL/ETA/OATELS
525 S Griffin St., Rm. 317
Dallas, TX 75202
Opitz.Steve@dol.gov

Region 4 covers Arkansas, Colorado, Louisiana, Montana, New Mexico, North Dakota, Oklahoma, South Dakota, Texas, Utah, and Wyoming.

Region 5

Regional Director
USDOL/ETA/OATELS
230 S. Dearborn St., Rm. 656
Chicago, IL 60604
Benewich.Terrence@dol.gov

Region 5 covers Illinois, Indiana, Iowa, Kansas, Michigan, Minnesota, Missouri, Nebraska, Ohio, and Wisconsin.

Region 6

Regional Director
USDOL/ETA/OATELS
71 Stevenson St., Ste. 815
San Francisco, CA 94105
Longeuay.Michael@dol.gov

Region 6 covers Alaska, Arizona, California, Hawaii, Idaho, Nevada, Oregon, and Washington.

U.S. Bureau of Apprenticeship and Training, State Offices

The U.S. Bureau of Apprenticeship and Training (USDL-BAT) maintains an office in each of the fifty states, as listed here. A person seeking to enroll for training in a particular state can contact his or her state office for information on how to do so. You can also view the list at www.doleta.gov/ATELS_bat/stateoffices.cfm.

Alabama

State Director
USDOL/ETA/OATELS-BAT
Medical Forum Bldg., Rm. 648
950 Twenty-second St. North
Birmingham, AL 35203

Alaska

State Director
USDOL/ETA/OATELS-BAT
605 W. Fourth Ave., Rm. G-30
Anchorage, AK 99501

Arizona

State Director
USDOL/ETA/OATELS-BAT
230 N. First Ave., Ste. 510
Phoenix, AZ 85025

Arkansas

State Director
USDOL/ETA/OATELS-BAT
Federal Bldg., Rm. 3507
700 W. Capitol St.
Little Rock, AR 72201

California

State Director
USDOL/ETA/OATELS-BAT
1301 Clay St., Ste. 1090-N
Oakland, CA 94612

Colorado

State Director
USDOL/ETA/OATELS-BAT
U.S. Custom House, Rm. 465
721 Nineteenth St.
Denver, CO 80202

Florida

State Director
USDOL/ETA/OATELS-BAT
400 W. Bay St., Ste. 934
P.O. Box 10
Jacksonville, FL 32202

Georgia

State Director
USDOL/ETA/OATELS-BAT
61 Forsyth St. SW, Rm. 6T80
Atlanta, GA 30303

Hawaii

State Director
61 Forsyth St. SW
300 Ala Moana Blvd., Rm. 5-117
Honolulu, HI 96850

Idaho

State Director
USDOL/ETA/OATELS-BAT
1150 N. Curtis Rd., Ste. 204
Boise, ID 83706

Illinois

State Director
USDOL/ETA/OATELS-BAT
230 S. Dearborn St., Rm. 656
Chicago, IL 60604

Indiana

State Director
USDOL/ETA/OATELS-BAT
Federal Bldg./U.S. Courthouse, Rm. 528
46 E. Ohio St.
Indianapolis, IN 46204

Iowa

State Director
USDOL/ETA/OATELS-BAT
Federal Bldg., Rm. 715-A
210 Walnut St.
Des Moines, IA 50309

Kansas

State Director
USDOL/ETA/OATELS-BAT
Federal Bldg., Rm. 247
444 SE Quincy St.
Topeka, KS 66683

Kentucky

State Director
USDOL/ETA/OATELS-BAT
Federal Bldg., Rm. 168
600 Martin Luther King Pl.
Louisville, KY 40202

Maryland

State Director
USDOL/ETA/OATELS-BAT
Federal Bldg., Rm. 430-B
31 Hopkins Plaza
Baltimore, MD 21201

Massachusetts

State Director
USDOL/ETA/OATELS-BAT
JFK Federal Bldg., Rm. E-370
Boston, MA 02203

Michigan

State Director
USDOL/ETA/OATELS-BAT
315 W. Allegan, Rm. 209
Lansing, MI 48933

Minnesota

State Director
USDOL/ETA/OATELS-BAT
Federal Bldg./U.S. Courthouse, Rm. 144
316 N. Robert St.
St. Paul, MN 55101

Mississippi

State Director
USDOL/ETA/OATELS-BAT
Federal Bldg., Ste. 515
100 W. Capitol St.
Jackson, MS 39269

Missouri

State Director
USDOL/ETA/OATELS-BAT
Robert A. Young Federal Bldg., Rm. 9, 102E
1222 Spruce St.
St. Louis, MO 63103

Nebraska

State Director
USDOL/ETA/OATELS-BAT
111 S. Eighteenth Plaza
Omaha, NE 68102

Nevada

State Director
USDOL/ETA/OATELS-BAT
600 S. Las Vegas Blvd., Ste. 520
Las Vegas, NV 89101

New Hampshire

State Director
USDOL/ETA/OATELS-BAT
Cleveland Bldg., Rm. 3703
55 Pleasant St.
Concord, NH 03301

New Jersey

State Director
USDOL/ETA/OATELS-BAT
Bldg. E, Third Fl.
485 Rte. 1 South
Iselin, NJ 08830

New Mexico

State Director
USDOL/ETA/OATELS-BAT
500 Fourth St. NW, Ste. 401
Albuquerque, NM 87102

New York

State Director
USDOL/ETA/OATELS-BAT
Leo O'Brien Federal Bldg., Rm. 809
North Pearl & Clinton Ave.
Albany, NY 12207

North Dakota

State Director
USDOL/ETA/OATELS-BAT
2500 W. Forty-Ninth St., Rm. 204
Sioux Falls, SD 57105

Ohio

State Director
USDOL/ETA/OATELS-BAT
200 N. High St., Rm. 605
Columbus, OH 43215

Oklahoma

State Director
USDOL/ETA/OATELS-BAT
1500 S. Midwest Blvd., Ste. 202
Midwest City, OK 73110

Oregon

State Director
USDOL/ETA/OATELS-BAT
256 Warner-Milne Rd., Rm. 3
Oregon City, OR 97045

Pennsylvania

State Director
USDOL/ETA/OATELS-BAT
Federal Bldg., Rm. 356
228 Walnut St.
Harrisburg, PA 17108

Rhode Island

State Director
USDOL/ETA/OATELS-BAT
Federal Bldg.
100 Hartford Ave.
Providence, RI 02909

South Carolina

State Director
USDOL/ETA/OATELS-BAT
Strom Thurmond Federal Bldg., Rm. 838
1835 Assembly St.
Columbia, SC 29201

South Dakota

State Director
USDOL/ETA/OATELS-BAT
Oxbow 1 Bldg.
2500 W. Forty-ninth St., Rm. 204
Sioux Falls, SD 57105

Tennessee

State Director
USDOL/ETA/OATELS-BAT
Airport Executive Plaza
1321 Murfreesboro Rd., Ste. 541
Nashville, TN 37210

Texas

State Director
USDOL/ETA/OATELS-BAT
300 E. Eighth St., Ste. 914
Austin, TX 78701

Utah

State Director
USDOL/ETA/OATELS-BAT
1600 W. 2200 South, Ste. 101
Salt Lake City, UT 84119

Virginia

State Director
USDOL/ETA/OATELS-BAT
Federal Bldg., Ste. 404
400 N. Eighth St.
Richmond, VA 23219

Washington

State Director
USDOL/ETA/OATELS-BAT
1111 Third Ave., Ste. 850
Seattle, WA 98101

West Virginia

State Director
USDOL/ETA/OATELS-BAT
One Bridge Pl., 2nd Fl.
10 Hale St.
Charleston, WV 25301

Wisconsin

State Director
USDOL/ETA/OATELS-BAT
740 Regent St., Ste. 104
Madison, WI 53715

Wyoming

State Director
USDOL/ETA/OATELS-BAT
American National Bank Bldg.
1912 Capitol Ave., Rm. 508
Cheyenne, WY 82001

Canada's Red Seal Progam

The Red Seal apprenticeship program oversees interprovincial standards and access to training through education, labor, or training departments in each province.

CCDA Executive Secretary
Human Resources and Skills Development Canada
Red Seal Secretariat
140 Promenade du Portage
Phase IV, 5th Fl.
Ottawa/Hull K1A 0J9
www.red-seal.ca

Alberta

Executive Director
Apprenticeship and Industry Training
7th Fl., Commerce Pl.
10155-102 St.
Edmonton, AB T5J 4L5
www.tradesecrets.org

British Columbia

VP Operations
Industry Training Authority
1223-13351 Commerce Pkwy.
Richmond, BC V6V 2X7
www.itabc.ca

Manitoba

Executive Director
Apprenticeship Branch
Advanced Education and Training
1010-401 York Ave.
Winnipeg, MB R3C 0P8
www.edu.gov.mb.ca/aet/apprent/index.htm

New Brunswick

Director
Apprenticeship & Occupational Development
470 York St.
1st Fl., Rm. 100, Chestnut Complex
Fredericton, NB E3B 5H1
www.aoc-acp.gnb.ca/home_eng.htm

Newfoundland and Labrador

Director, Division of Institutional and Industrial Education
Department of Education
P.O. Box 8700, 4th Fl.
Confederation Bldg., West Block
Prince Philip Dr.
St. John's, NL A1B 4J6
www.gov.nf.ca/edu/post/app.htm

Northwest Territories

Director of College & Career Development
Department of Education, Culture, and Employment Programs
Government of the Northwest Territories
Box 1320
Yellowknife, NT X1A 2L9
www.ece.gov.nt.ca

Nova Scotia

Director, Apprenticeship Training and Skill Development
Department of Education
P.O. Box 578
Halifax, NS B3J 2S9
www.apprenticeship.ednet.ns.ca

Nunavut

Director
Adult Learning & Post Secondary Services
Box 390
Arviat, NU X0C 0E0
www.gov.nu.ca/education/eng/index.htm

Ontario

Director, Workplace Support Services Branch
Ministry of Training, Colleges, and Universities
17th Fl., Mowat Block
900 Bay St.
Toronto, ON M7A 1L2
www.edu.gov.on.ca/eng/welcome.html

Prince Edward Island

Manager of Apprenticeship
Department of Education
Continuing Education and Training
P.O. Box 2000
Charlottetown, PE C1A 7N8
www.apprenticeship.pe.ca

Quebec

Director of Apprenticeship
Emploi-Québec
Direction de l'apprentissage et du développement des comptences en milieu de travail
800 Tour de la Place Victoria, 27th Fl.
C.P. 100
Montréal, QC H4Z 1B7
http://emploiquebec.net/anglais/index.htm

Saskatchewan

Director
Apprenticeship & Trade Certification Commission
2140 Hamilton St.
Regina, SK S4P 3V7
www.saskapprenticeship.ca

Yukon

Assistant Deputy Minister
Department of Education
Government of the Yukon Territory
P.O. Box 2703
Whitehorse, YK Y1A 2C6
www.education.gov.yk.ca

Appendix C

Trade Associations

THERE ARE TRADE associations of building trades management and trade associations of building trades workers. This appendix lists both, as they relate to carpentry and its allied trades. Several of these associations have programs to assist prospective workers who want to enter their trades.

Associated Builders and Contractors
4250 N. Fairfax Dr., 9th Fl.
Arlington, VA 22203
www.abc.org

Associated General Contractors of America
2300 Wilson Blvd., Ste. 400
Arlington, VA 22201
www.agc.org

Association of Union Constructors
1501 Lee Hwy., Ste. 202
Arlington, VA 22209
www.nea-online.org

Association of the Wall and Ceiling Industry
803 W. Broad St., Ste. 600
Falls Church, VA 22046
www.awci.org

Building Trades Association
www.buildingtrades.com

Canadian Association of Women in Construction
www.cawic.ca

Canadian Construction Association
75 Albert St., Ste. 400
Ottawa, ON K1P 5E7
www.cca-acc.com/home.html

Canadian Homebuilders' Association
www.chba.ca

Floor Covering Installation Contractors Association
7439 Millwood Dr.
West Bloomfield, MI 48322
www.fcica.com

Home Builders Institute (National Association of Home
Builders)
1201 Fifteenth St. NW, 6th Fl.
Washington, DC 20005
www.hbi.org

International Union of Painters and Allied Trades
1750 New York Ave. NW
Washington, DC 20006
www.iupat.org

National Association of Women in Construction
327 S. Adams St.
Fort Worth, TX 76104
www.nawic.org/contact.htm

United Brotherhood of Carpenters and Joiners of America
101 Constitution Ave. NW
Washington, DC 20001
www.carpenters.org

Appendix D

Academic Programs

The programs included here offer training in some aspect of carpentry: residential construction, commercial construction, cabinetmaking, millwork, and even boatbuilding. Scope and intensity vary, from six-month certificate programs to associate's degrees and beyond. In addition to these resources, many school districts and vocational/technical schools offer classroom instruction to complement carpentry apprenticeships, as well as isolated introductory woodworking courses that would allow you to sample the trade without commitment. Check with your local school district or career office for opportunities.

U.S. Schools

Alabama

Bishop State Community College (Mobile):
www.bishop.edu
Gadsden State Community College (Gadsden):
www.gadsdenstate.edu

J. F. Ingram State Technical College (Deatsville):
www.ingram.cc.al.us
Northwest Shoals Community College (Muscle Shoals):
www.nwscc.cc.al.us/occupational/occupational.html
Shelton State Community College (Tuscaloosa):
www.sheltonstate.edu

Alaska

Ilisagvik College (Barrow): www.ilisagvik.edu

Arizona

Central Arizona College (Coolidge): www.centralaz.edu

California

College of the Redwoods (Eureka): www.redwoods.edu
El Camino College (Torrance): www.elcamino.edu
Fresno City College: www.fresnocitycollege.edu
Laney College (Oakland): http://laney.peralta.edu
Long Beach City College: www.lbcc.edu
Los Angeles Trade Technical College: www.lattc.edu
Palomar College (San Marcos): www.palomar.edu
San Joaquin Delta College (Stockton):
www.deltacollege.edu
Sierra College (Rocklin): www.sierracollege.edu

Florida

Erwin Technical Center (Tampa): http://erwintech.org
First Coast Technical Institute (St. Augustine):
www.fcti.org

Florida Community College at Jacksonville: www.fccj.edu
Lee County High Tech Center Central (Myers):
  www.hightechcentral.org
Mid Florida Tech (Orlando): www.mft.ocps.net
North Florida Community College (Madison):
  www.nfcc.edu
Okaloosa Applied Technology Center (Ft. Walton Beach):
  www.okaloosa.k12.fl.us/oatc
Pinellas Technical Education Center (Clearwater):
  www.myptec.org
Washington-Holmes Technical Center (Chipley):
  www.firn.edu/schools/washington/whtech

Georgia

Albany Technical College: www.albanytech.edu
Altamaha Technical College (Jesup):
  www.altamahatech.org
Atlanta Technical College: www.atlantatech.org
Columbus Technical College: www.columbustech.org
Gwinnett Technical College (Lawrenceville):
  www.gwinnettechnicalcollege.com
Moultrie Technical College: www.moultrietech.edu

Hawaii

Hawaii Community College (Hilo):
  www.hawcc.hawaii.edu
Honolulu Community College:
  http://honolulu.hawaii.edu

Idaho

College of Southern Idaho (Twin Falls): www.csi.edu

North Idaho College (Coeur d'Alene): www.nic.edu

Illinois

Dawson Technical Institute at Kennedy-King College (Chicago): www.ccc.edu

John A. Logan College (Carterville): www.jal.cc.il.us

Southwestern Illinois College (Belleville): www.swic.edu

Iowa

Iowa Lakes Community College (Emmetsburg): www.ilcc.cc.ia.us

Kirkwood Community College (Cedar Rapids): www.kirkwood.edu

Northeast Iowa Community College (Calmar, Peosta): www.nicc.edu

Northwest Iowa Community College (Sheldon): www.nwicc.com

Southwestern Community College (Red Oak): www.swcciowa.edu

Western Iowa Tech Community College (Sioux City): www.witcc.com

Kansas

Coffeeville Community College (Columbus): www.coffeyville.edu

Flint Hills Technical College (Emporia): www.fhtc.net

Kansas City Area Technical School: www.kckats.com

Manhattan Area Technical College: www.matc.net

North Central Kansas Technical College (Beloit): www.ncktc.tec.ks.us

Northwest Kansas Technical College (Goodland): www.nwktc.org

Salina Area Technical School: www.salinatech.com

Southwest Kansas Technical School (Liberal): www.usd480.net/swkts/main.html

Wichita Area Technical College: www.watc.edu

Kentucky

Ashland Community and Technical College: www.ashland.kctcs.edu

Elizabethtown Community and Technical College: www.elizabethtown.kctcs.edu

Hazard Community and Technical College: www.hazard.kctcs.edu

Kentucky Community and Technical College System (Versailles): www.jefferson.kctcs.edu

Madisonville Community College: www.madcc.kctcs.net

Owensboro Community and Technical College: www.octc.kctcs.edu

Somerset Community College (London): www.somerset.kctcs.edu

West Kentucky Community and Technical College (Paducah): www.westkentucky.kctcs.edu

Louisiana

Louisiana Technical College (Bogalusa, Harvey, Leesville, Minden, Morgan City, New Iberia, New Roads, Shreveport, Thibodaux, Winnfield): www.ltc.edu

Maine

The Landing School (Kennebunkport): www.thelandingschool.org
Northern Maine Community College (Presque Isle): www.nmcc.edu
Southern Maine Community College (South Portland): www.smccme.edu

Massachusetts

Blue Hills Regional Technical School (Canton): www.bluehills.org
North Bennet Street School (Boston): www.nbss.org

Michigan

Northern Michigan University (Marquette): www.nmu.edu

Minnesota

Alexandria Technical College: http://web.alextech.edu
Hennepin Technical College (Plymouth): www.hennepintech.edu
Lake Superior College (Duluth): www.lsc.mnscu.edu

Mesabi Range Community and Technical College
    (Virginia): www.mesabirange.mnscu.edu
Minnesota State College, Southeast Technical (Red Wing,
    Winona): www.southeastmn.edu
Minnesota West Community and Technical College
    (Pipestone): www.mnwest.edu
Northwest Technical College (Bemidji): www.ntcmn.edu
Ridgewater College (Willmar):
    www.ridgewater.mnscu.edu
Riverland Community College (Austin):
    www.riverland.edu
Rochester Community and Technical College:
    www.rctc.edu
Saint Cloud Technical College: www.sctc.edu
Saint Paul College: www.saintpaul.edu
South Central College (Faribault): www.sctc.mnscu.edu
Summit Academy OIC (Minneapolis): www.saoic.org

Mississippi

Coahoma Community College (Clarksdale):
    www.ccc.cc.ms.us
East Central Community College (Decatur):
    www.eccc.cc.ms.us
Hinds Community College (Raymond, Utica):
    www.hindscc.edu
Meridian Community College: www.mcc.cc.ms.us

Missouri

Cape Girardeau Career and Technology Center:
    www.cape.k12.mo.us/cc

Cass Career Center (Harrisonville):
www.casscareercenter.com
Grand River Technical School (Chillicothe): www.grts.org
Hannibal Career and Technical Center:
www.hannibal.tec.mo.us
North Central Missouri College (Trenton):
www.ncmc.cc.mo.us
Northland Career Center (Platte City):
www.northlandcareercenter.com
Ranken Technical College (St. Louis): www.ranken.org
Saline County Career Center (Marshall):
www.marshallschools.com/sccc

Montana

University of Montana, Helena College of Technology:
www.umhelena.edu

Nebraska

Nebraska Indian Community College (Macy):
www.thenicc.edu
Southeast Community College (Beatrice, Lincoln,
Milford): www.southeast.edu

New Jersey

Middlesex County Vocational and Technical Schools:
www.mcvts.net
Ocean County Vocational Schools: www.ocvts.org
Technical Institute of Camden County: www.ccts.tec.nj.us

New Mexico

Central New Mexico Community College (Albuquerque): www.cnm.edu

Crownpoint Institute of Technology: http://cit.cc.nm.us

New York

Genesee Valley Boces (Batavia, Mt. Morris): www.gvboces.org

SUNY Delhi: www.delhi.edu

North Carolina

Alamance Community College (Graham): www.alamance.cc.nc.us

Asheville-Buncombe Technical Community College (Asheville, Enka, Madison): www.abtech.edu

Bladen Community College (Dublin): www.bladen.cc.nc.us

Cape Fear Community College (Wilmington): http://cfcc.edu

College of the Albemarle (Elizabeth City): www.albemarle.cc.nc.us

Fayetteville Technical Community College: www.faytechcc.edu

Forsyth Tech Community College (Winston Salem): www.forsythtech.edu

Guilford Technical Community College (Jamestown): http://technet.gtcc.cc.nc.us

Mayland Community College (Spruce Pine): www.mayland.cc.nc.us

McDowell Technical Community College (Marion):
www.mcdowelltech.cc.nc.us
Surry Community College (Dobson): www.surry.edu
Vance-Granville Community College (Henderson):
www.vgcc.edu

North Dakota

Bismarck State College: www.bismarckstate.edu
Cankdeska Cikana Community College (Fort Totten):
www.littlehoop.edu
Turtle Mountain Community College (Belcourt):
www.turtle-mountain.cc.nd.us
United Tribes Technical College (Bismarck): www.uttc.edu

Ohio

Cleveland Municipal School District:
www.cmsdnet.net/adulted
Eastland-Fairfield Career and Technical Schools
(Groveport): www.eastland.k12.oh.us/adult
Great Oaks (Cincinnati): www.greatoaks.com
Portage Lakes Career Center (Green): www.plcc.k12.oh.us

Oklahoma

Central Tech (Drumright): www.ctechok.org
Francis Tuttle Technology Center (Oklahoma City):
www.francistuttle.com
Great Plains Technology Center (Lawton):
www.gptech.org

Kiamichi Technology Center (Atoka):
www.kiamichi-atoka.tec.ok.us
Kiamichi Technology Center (McAlester):
www.kiamichi-mcalester.tec.ok.us
Kiamichi Technology Center (Poteau):
www.kiamichi-poteau.tec.ok.us
Kiamichi Technology Center (Stigler):
www.kiamichi-stigler.tec.ok.us
Kiamichi Technology Center (Talihina):
www.kiamichi-talihina.tec.ok.us
Metro Technology Centers (Oklahoma City):
www.metrotech.org
Southern Oklahoma Technology Center (Ardmore):
www.sotc.org

Pennsylvania

Community College of Allegheny County: www.ccac.edu
Delaware County Community College: www.dccc.edu
Orleans Technical Institute (Philadelphia):
www.orleanstech.edu
Pennsylvania College of Technology (Williamsport):
www.pct.edu
Schuylkill Intermediate Unit 29 (Marlin): www.iu29.org
Thaddeus Stevens College of Technology (Lancaster):
www.stevenstech.org
Triangle Tech (Bethlehem, DuBois, Erie, Greensburg,
Sunbury): www.triangle-tech.com

Rhode Island

New England Institute of Technology (Warwick):
www.neit.edu

South Carolina

Bob Jones University (Greenville): www.bju.edu
Greenville Technical College: http://greenvilletech.com

South Dakota

Lake Area Technical Institute (Watertown):
www.lakeareatech.edu
Western Dakota Technical Institute (Rapid City):
www.westerndakotatech.org

Texas

Austin Community College: www.austincc.edu
McLennan Community College (Waco):
www.mclennan.edu

Utah

Bridgerland Applied Technology College (Logan):
http://batc.edu
Ogden-Weber Applied Technology College (Ogden):
www.owatc.com
Salt Lake Community College: www.slcc.edu
Southern Utah University (Cedar City): www.suu.edu
Utah Valley State College (Orem): www.uvsc.edu

Washington

Bates Technical College (Tacoma): www.bates.ctc.edu

Edmonds Community College (Lynnwood):
www.edcc.edu

Grays Harbor College (Aberdeen): http://ghc.ctc.edu

Green River Community College (Auburn):
www.greenriver.edu

Northwest School of Wooden Boatbuilding (Port
Townsend): www.nwboatschool.org

Peninsula College (Port Angeles): www.pc.ctc.edu

Seattle Central Community College:
www.seattlecentral.org

Spokane Community College: www.scc.spokane.edu

Walla Walla Community College: www.wwcc.edu

Wisconsin

Chippewa Valley Technical College (Eau Claire):
www.cvtc.edu

College of Menominee Nation (Green Bay, Keshena):
www.menominee.edu

Milwaukee Area Technical College: http://matc.edu

Northeast Wisconsin Technical College (Green Bay):
www.nwtc.edu

Waukesha County Technical College: www.wctc.edu

Wyoming

Laramie County Community College: www.lccc.cc.wy.us

Canadian Schools

Alberta

Northern Alberta Institute of Technology (Edmonton):
www.nait.ca
Northern Lakes College (Slave Lake):
www.northernlakescollege.ca
Red Deer College: www.rdc.ab.ca

British Columbia

College of New Caledonia (Prince George): www.cnc.bc.ca
College of the Rockies (Cranbrook): www.cotr.bc.ca
Discovery Community College (Campbell River):
www.discoverycommunitycollege.com
Kwantlen University College (Newton): www.kwantlen.ca
Malaspina University-College (Cowichan, Nanaimo,
Powell River): www.mala.ca
North Island Community College (Port Alberni–Tebo
Vocational Centre): www.nic.bc.ca
Northern Lights College (Chetwynd, Dawson Creek):
http://nlc.bc.ca
Northwest Community College (Terrace):
www.nwcc.bc.ca
Selkirk College (Nelson–Silver King): http://selkirk.ca
University College of the Fraser Valley (Abbotsford):
www.ucfv.ca

Manitoba

Red River College of Applied Arts, Science, and
Technology (Winnipeg): www.rrc.mb.ca

New Brunswick

New Brunswick Community College (Miramichi,
Moncton, Woodstock): www.nbcc.ca

Newfoundland and Labrador

Academy Canada (Corner Brook, St. John's):
www.academycanada.com
College of the North Atlantic (Clarenville, Happy
Valley–Goose Bay): www.cna.nl.ca

Nova Scotia

Nova Scotia Community College (Stellarton):
www.nscc.ca

Nunavut

Nunavut Arctic College (Kitikmeot, Kivalliq, Nunatta):
www.nac.nu.ca

Ontario

Algonquin College (Ottawa): www.algonquincollege.com
Cambrian College (Sudbury): www.cambrianc.on.ca
Conestoga College (Kitchener): www.conestogac.on.ca
Fanshawe College (London): www.fanshawec.on.ca

Humber College Institute of Technology and Advanced
Learning (Humber North):
http://postsecondary.humber.ca
Niagara College (Welland): http://niagarac.on.ca

Saskatchewan

North West Regional College (North Battleford):
www.nwrc.sk.ca
Prairie West Regional College (Outlook): www.pwrc.sk.ca
Saskatchewan Institute of Applied Science and Technology
(Palliser, Woodland): www.siast.sk.ca

Glossary

Acoustical material   Composition board and other materials manufactured in sections and placed upon the ceiling or walls of a structure to absorb sounds or reduce sound reflection and echo.

Acoustics   Pertaining to sound.

Agreement, collective   A contract (agreement and contract are used interchangeably) between a union, acting as bargaining agent, and an employer, covering wages, hours, working conditions, and fringe benefits.

Anchor bolt   Bolt joining a house's frame with the foundation it rests on.

ANSI   American National Standards Institute (www.ansi.org).

Apprentice   A learner who is under supervision with regard to work experience, often coupled with related classroom studies.

Completion of the required years of apprenticeship training leads to journeyman status.

Area differential   Variation in wage rates between areas or regions of the country for same work. Also called *geographical differential.*

Band joist   The board in a flooring system that runs perpendicular to the joists and supports them.

Backing board   A term used in the installation of acoustical materials. It is applied either to panels or furring strips placed on walls, partitions, and ceilings before acoustical tiles or other facings are applied.

Bar   In acoustical tile installation, the term is applied to metal bars to which the tiles are affixed.

Beam pocket   The notch atop a load-bearing wall to hold a beam in place.

Biscuit   A hidden joint made using a biscuit saw, which cuts matching slots in the respective boards' edges and joins them using "biscuits," flat wood tabs glued into the slots.

Blue-collar workers   Production and maintenance workers and construction workers as compared with office and professional workers, who wear "white collars."

Blueprint   A reproduction of an architect's or designer's plans by a photographic process in white lines on a bright blue background.

Building system   Another term for systems construction, whereby materials, labor, prefabricated units, and so forth are scheduled for maximum efficiency in time and costs.

Butt joint   A simple joint in which the two boards do not interlock, but merely abut one another and rely on some other structural element for support.

Calibration   The markings on an instrument in degrees, meters, and so on, that indicate a unit of measurement.

Cantilever   A board or frame that extends beyond the structure below and whose load sits over the overhanging section.

Casual work   Work that occurs irregularly, on no fixed schedule.

Catwalk   A support timber running along the center of a truss's bottom chord.

Channel   A term used in acoustical tile installation that refers to the angled rods and bars supporting the tiles.

Component   A distinct part of a whole, as a transistor is a component of a radio; a stove, a component of a kitchen.

Contractor   A person or company that agrees by contract to do certain work under specified conditions and prices.

Craft   An occupation or trade requiring a particular ability or skill.

Craftsperson   A person who practices a particular trade or skill.

Decking   Materials used for flooring (usually in an exposed area), as, for example, the roadway of a bridge and the flat-floored roofless area adjoining a house.

Drywall   Panels of gypsum board, fiber board, plywood, or gypsum plaster erected as manufactured in a "dry operation," as opposed to a "wet wall" or wet plaster construction.

Estimator   One who calculates the amount of materials needed, the labor necessary, and the general costs of a construction job or installation work.

Fabrication   Anything constructed from standardized parts. In construction work, the term is usually applied to components that come to a construction site already prepared for installation.

Face nailing   Setting a nail that will be exposed on the face of the finished work. The opposite of blind nailing.

Finish work   The fine, sometimes decorative, work involved in the final stages of construction, installation, or remodeling, usually of a more highly skilled nature.

Fire blocking   That type of construction work in which fire hazards are reduced by applying wood blocks between studs to prevent "chimney effect" in the event of fire. The blocks stifle the flow of air and help to smother a fire.

Fixture   Something that is fixed in place; for example, a wall cabinet or a ceiling light.

Foreman   A chief and, usually, a specially trained or more experienced worker, who directs the activity of a work crew.

Form   The framing built of wood, metal, or other material that serves as a form or mold for poured concrete.

Frame   Something composed of parts fitted together and united. In construction, this usually applies to a wooden frame.

Framing   The process of putting together the skeleton parts of a building. Also, the rough lumber work on a structure, such as flooring, roofing, framework, and partitions.

Free form A form that has no fixed specifications; usually a variation from a straight line.

Fringe benefits Employment benefits granted by an employer or obtained by labor-management contract that are received over and above the basic wage rate; for example, hospitalization insurance and tool allowance.

Furring The application of thin wood, brick, or metal to joists, studs, or walls to form a level surface or an air space. To build a separate wall offset from the main wall. Also, the materials used in such work.

Hand/feet rule A precaution in ladder safety calling for at least two hands and one foot or two feet and one hand on the ladder at all times.

Hanger A wire or bar used for suspending one object from another, as pipes are hung from a ceiling, or a stirruplike drop support attached to a wall to carry the end of a beam.

Hypotenuse In a right triangle, the side found across from the 90-degree angle, also the longest side.

Inspector A person who is employed to examine a project, a work site, or an activity to make sure that standards or policies are being carried out.

Jack leg A slang term for an amateur or unskilled carpenter or other worker.

Joiner A wood craftsperson who constructs joints or wood connections. Usually a term applied to the workers in shops who construct doors, windows, and other fitted parts of a structure.

Joint committee   In this instance, a training committee made up of labor and management, with public officials who serve as consultants or nonvoting members.

Jointer   Any of various tools used in making joints; also, a person who unites materials with joints.

Joist   A horizontal beam used with others as a support for a floor, ceiling, or roof.

Journeyman   A person who has completed his or her apprenticeship and is entitled to the highest minimum wage rate established for his or her job classification.

Jurisdiction   The area of work or group of employees for which a union claims the rights to bargain collectively.

Laminated   Composed of layers of wood, or other building materials bonded or impregnated by resins or other adhesives. Plywood, for example, is created of laminated sheets of wood veneer.

Lath   Any material that is secured to studs or joists and on which plaster is applied.

Lathe   A machine in which wood or other solid material is rotated about a horizontal axis and shaped by a fixed cutting tool; also, the action of cutting or shaping with a lathe.

Layout work   The ability to read blueprints and specifications and layout and direct work for others to follow.

Machining   Turning, shaping, planing, milling, or otherwise finishing or reducing a product using machine-operated tools.

Manual skills   Those skills performed by hand that require or use physical skills and energy.

Masonry   The art or occupation of a mason, that is, bricklaying, stonework, building with concrete blocks, cinder blocks, and so forth.

Masonry nailing   Driving nails into concrete blocks, bricks, and similar building materials.

Millwork   Finished carpentry work or work completed in a woodworking mill, such as assembled windows, window frames, doors, and door frames.

Millwright   A subsection of the carpentry craft; a worker who installs machinery and related components, such as conveyor systems, in mills, industrial complexes, and power plants.

Modular   Constructed with standardized units or dimensions for easy assembly and a variety of uses.

On-the-job training   Training for higher skills while employed in a particular craft or occupation; one is paid wages or a salary while one learns.

Partition   Something that divides; in construction, usually an interior wall separating rooms. Used for aesthetics, partitions do not support any of the larger structure.

Pile   A long, slender shaft, usually of wood, steel, or reinforced concrete, that is driven into the ground to bear weight.

Pile driver   A machine for driving down piles with a pile hammer or a steam or air hammer; also, the operator of a pile driver.

Pitch   The degree of slope of a rafter, roof, or other component of a framework.

Planer   A machine for smoothing or shaping a wood surface.

Planing mill   An array of planers used for giving a smooth or decorated surface to wood.

Power tool   Any tool operated by a motor, usually electric.

Preapprenticeship   Special training now being offered to prepare young persons to qualify for the actual apprenticeship program.

Prefabricate   To make parts in a factory so that construction consists of assembling at the erection site.

Premium pay   "Top pay," or pay above what is usually expected.

Pro rata   Proportionately, according to some factor that has been exactly figured.

Rafter   Any of the parallel beams that support a roof.

Reinforced concrete   Concrete in which steel or other materials are used to reinforce strength.

Resilient   In construction, the term is applied to various types of floor covers that are somewhat elastic in application and installation, as with vinyl tiles.

Rough framing   The skeleton of a structure, usually built with lumber of standard dimensions. Also applies to the work involved in erecting such a structure.

Router   A machine with a revolving vertical spindle and cutter for milling out the surface of wood or metal.

Sander   A machine that sands surfaces to smooth, clean, or roughen them in preparation for finishing.

Scaffolding An array of temporary or movable platforms for workers to stand or sit on while working at a height above the floor or ground.

Scribe To mark a line by cutting or scratching with a pointed instrument.

Seam A line, groove, or ridge formed by the abutment of edges.

Seasonality The effect of weather and temperature on working conditions.

Sheathing The first covering of boards or waterproofing material on the outside wall of a frame house or on a timber roof.

Shop course A course of study and training in which the student actually uses tools of the trade or craft.

Shoring The act of supporting with props or retaining walls; also, the system of props and braces that act as supports or shores for concrete formwork.

Siding Material that forms the exposed surface of outside walls of frame buildings. It is nailed over the sheathing.

Skeleton frame The basic framework of main support timbers in a structure.

Sound insulation Insulation designed to trap and/or direct sound waves for acoustical control.

Spline A thin piece of corrugated metal or a wooden strip used in construction to strengthen wood joints. It is driven into the two pieces of wood at the joint.

Stage   A scaffold or platform for workers, usually one that can be raised or lowered by ropes and pulleys.

Stake out   To mark on the ground or other surface the limits and main points of the foundation of a structure before its erection. This is usually done by driving stakes into the ground.

Standard   Something set up and established by authority, custom, or general consent as a model or example.

Stiffener   Anything added to a material to give it more stability and strength.

Stock   Raw material from which something is produced.

Structural steel   Steel used in producing a metal framework for a building or other structure.

Stud   One of the smaller uprights in the framing of the walls of a building to which sheathing, paneling, or laths are fastened.

Subcontractor   A company or individual who enters into an agreement with a general contractor. The subcontractor usually agrees to do certain skilled work on a building. Plumbing, heating, and electrical work are subcontracted to companies that specialize in one kind of work.

Subflooring   The basic lumber or panels laid over joists before flooring is applied.

Superintendent   A supervisor on a construction job who directs the foremen and their work crews.

Tee   A wood or metal joint with an abutting piece set at right angles as in a capital T.

Thermal insulation   Material used in building construction for protection from heat or cold.

Tolerance   The allowable deviation from a standard; the range of variation permitted in maintaining a specified dimension in materials or in construction.

Transit   An optical device used in land surveying and staking out foundations for construction.

Trim   The final, finished woodwork of a structure. The term is also used in reference to painting and decorating.

Veneer   A thin sheet of wood or other material, sometimes used as the facing on cabinets and other wood installations or assembled in sheets to form plywood.

Wage rate   The rate, established by contract or custom, that is used as the standard of pay for work done.

Wage scale   The listing of wages, highest to lowest, that shows comparative pay for particular job classifications.

Wood turner   One whose occupation is shaping wood by means of a lathe.

About the Author

Roger Sheldon has served as the communications director of the United Brotherhood of Carpenters and Joiners of America and has worked as an editor for the Brotherhood's magazine, *The Carpenter*, including as the managing editor and also as an editorial consultant. He has served as an editorial advisor to several labor organizations and has done special work for the United States Department of Labor. In the early 1960s, he served as information officer for President John F. Kennedy's Commission on the Status of Women. And, for more than a decade, Mr. Sheldon was vice president and editorial director of Merkle Press, Inc., of Washington, DC.

A native of Baton Rouge, Louisiana, Sheldon graduated from Louisiana State University with a degree in journalism.

The author would like to thank Brad Crawford for his assistance in preparing this revision.